Africa in Print

OTHER TITLES BY
JAMES AND CLARE CURREY

Letters from South Africa
January 1963 to July 1964
By Clare and James Currey

From Sharpeville to Rivonia
July 1959–July 1964
With Clare Currey

Africa Writes Back
The African Writers Series
and the Launch of African Literature

The New African with *Cape Escape*
With Randolph Vigne

A Mill on the Beane
Three Families on a Venture

James Currey

Africa in Print

MEMOIR

OPS

Published in 2025 by Oxford Publishing Services.

Copyright © James Currey 2025.

The right of James Currey to be identified as author of the book has been asserted in accordance with the Copyright, Designs and Patents Act 1988. Images © Clare and James Currey. Cover images © Financial Times.

All rights reserved. No part of this publication may be reproduced, stored in a retrieval system, or transmitted in any form or by any means – electronic, mechanical, photocopying, recording or otherwise – without the prior written permission of the author, except in the case of brief quotations embodied in critical articles or reviews.

A catalogue record for this book is available from the British Library.

ISBN: 978 1 0686789 5 0

Copyedited and typeset in Garamond by Oxford Publishing Services.
Printed by Holywell Press Ltd, Oxford.

Dedication

Hannah Ella Martha Hattie

Contents

Acknowledgements	ix
Main Dates	x
Families	xii
Family Tree	xvi

ONE
All the Fun of a War — 1

TWO
To Oxford — 33

THREE
Oxford University Press & South Africa — 46

FOUR
Just in Time for the Revolution — 63

FIVE
One Man One Vote — 80

SIX
The New African — 85

SEVEN
A Swing through West Africa — 92

EIGHT
With Clare to the Cape — 96

NINE
The 90-Day Police State — 100

TEN
Husbands in the Dock — 103

CONTENTS

ELEVEN
Great Trek to Central Africa — 106

TWELVE
James Leaps off Thorstream — 108

THIRTEEN
Escape from South Africa — 111

FOURTEEN
Thornhill Square, Caledonian Road — 133

FIFTEEN
African Writers Series — 137

SIXTEEN
The Establishment of African Literature — 139

SEVENTEEN
Key African Writers — 148

EIGHTEEN
Arab Authors — 166

NINETEEN
Caribbean Writers Series — 167

TWENTY
I Capture my Heinemann Titles — 171

TWENTY-ONE
James Currey Publishers Founded — 181

TWENTY-TWO
Lockdown for the Plague — 199

Index — 213

Acknowledgements

I have written this book first of all for my grand-daughters Hannah, Ella, Martha and Hattie. Hal and Sophie and Tamsin Currey have helped me to recall and secure my memory.

My carers John Ashman and Rose Barros have kept me well fed and healthy as I have written this book. They have driven and wheeled me to concerts, lectures and interesting occasions round Oxford and taken me to the Mill. Rose has now been helping me for more than five years. The first time she drove me was to Southwark Cathedral to become a Fellow of the Royal Society of Literature.

My neighbours have kept me in touch with a wider world. Karin Fremer is a book designer for the splendid Thames and Hudson and has laid out a book on the Finnish designers Marimekko. Joe Chamberlin has made television series on the Arab World and on Kent.

Lucy Slade has been a link with my memory of her mother Joanna Cacanas.

I am grateful to Selina Cohen for her splendid index.

I hope that from these pages it will be clear how Clare was vital to the success of James Currey Publishers.

Main Dates

1932	Ralph Nixon Currey marries Helen Estella Martin
1934	R. N. Currey appointed at Colchester Royal Grammar School (CRGS)
1936	James Currey, born Colchester, 6 September
1940	Andrew Currey, James's brother, born Colchester
1948	James attends Kingswood School, Westwood
1950	James attends School House, Kingswood
1953	GCSE results – nine passes
1955	A levels – history, English and French
1956	James goes to Wadham College, Oxford to read Modern History, where he becomes the features editor for *Isis* and the president of the Oxford International Committee
1957	James meets Clare Wilson, St Anne's College, Oxford, on 11 May
1958	BA Modern History, 2nd Class
	September: trainee at Oxford University Press, Amen House, London
1959	July: James moves to Cape Town to join Oxford University Press
1962	July on leave to London via West Africa
	Married Catherine Clare Wilson, 21 December
1963	2 January: Arrived in Cape Town with Clare
1964	9 July: James buys cabin for himself on *Thorstream* to enable Randolph Vigne to escape to Canada
	11 July: Clare and James fly to London via Rome
	September: James joins OUP's Overseas Education Department at Amen House

MAIN DATES

1965	OUP. Take over Rex Collings's Africa list including Three Crowns series (with Soyinka, first Nobel Prize for Literature from Africa)
1965	Hal born, 27 April
1967	1 April: joined Alan Hill and Keith Sambrook, Heinemann Educational Books (HEB), London to run African and Caribbean publishing under Keith Sambrook
	African Writers Series (Editorial Adviser Chinua Achebe), 270 titles added with Aig Higo in Ibadan Nigeria and Henry Chakava in Nairobi
1967	Tamsin born, 6 September
1971	Henry Chakava joins HEB (EA) Nairobi as editor
1984	Heinemann has four owners in five years
	James Currey demands redundancy because AWS takeover reduced his list to two titles a year
1985	12 January: Clare and I found James Currey Publishers, Islington
1988	James Currey Publishers move to Oxford with new partner Douglas Johnson
2000	Award: African Studies Association US
2008	James Currey Publishers imprint sold to Boydell & Brewer, Woodbridge
2009	Distinguished Africanist Award ASAUK
2015	Enstooled: Pan African Writers Association
2016	Clare died, 26 April (born 15 November 1936)
2024	Elected Fellow of the Royal Society of Literature

Families

Granddaughter Ella said
'We don't know what granny and you did during your lives.'

James Currey

I, James Martin Currey, put off being born as expected at the end of August and waited until 6 September 1936, which was in the new school year. Tamsin was born on 6 September 1967 and was to be my best birthday present ever. Our birthdays were always a nuisance for us and our parents, for they meant that we had to take our public exams twice.

The name Currey

The spelling 'Curry' is much more common as it is derived from 'curragh', which is Celtic for a bog. The name CURREY came from Weardale. The dale ran up into the Pennines and the road passed down to Cumbria where my grandfather John Currey was born in 1871. All along the road there were davits running at an angle, which allowed trucks full of lead ore to be dragged out from the mountainside by pit ponies. The Curreys specialised in breeding those ponies. The chapels were mostly Methodist. My Currey grandfather told me how at the age of 14 he had led the ponies under the sea at Maryport. He became a local preacher and so managed to escape from mining to a Methodist college and to train as a missionary to go out to Africa, where he married Edith Vinnicombe from a Devonshire family. The spelling 'Currey' is much more common in South Africa. Ronald Currey was headmaster of St Andrew's, which was one of South Africa's best regarded private boarding schools. R. N. Currey found it annoying when R. Currey was credited with his poetry. The most famous was Tom Currey who was secretary to Rhodes himself — but he was no relation.

Martin family

There are many Martins in western Cornwall and our Methodist family farmed near St Austell. My other grandfather J. P. Martin (John Percival) also went out to South Africa as a Methodist missionary. He was engaged to Nancy Mann but they were only allowed to marry after he had served for five years among the gold miners at Pilgrim's Rest. Helen Estella (known as Stella) was born at Roodepoort in the Transvaal on 18 July 1907.

R. N. Currey: poet

Ralph Currey had spent his first 14 years in South Africa and so became known as a South African poet under his writing name of R. N. Currey. He was born at Mafeking in 1906. His parents were John and Edith Currey (née Vinnicombe). They looked after the Wesleyan Methodist missionary chapel in the African location. The town chapel for whites and coloureds was run by J. P. and Nancy Martin (née Mann). So Ralph and Stella knew one another as children. Ralph was sent away to Kingswood School in Bath, which John Wesley had founded in 1848. He had read history at Wadham College, Oxford where his tutor was the biographer Lord David Cecil.

After the reformation of the monasteries, education had to be provided by town grammar schools. In 1934, my father felt himself fortunate during the depression to be taken on to teach English and history at Colchester Royal Grammar School (CRGS) founded during the reigns of Henry VIII and Elizabeth I.

His first collection *Tiresias* was published in 1940 by the renowned Oxford University Press. One day Dylan Thomas turned to Ralph on a traffic island in front of the BBC and, after reciting his poem *Pelican, St James's Park*, asked if it was he who had written it. T. S. Eliot said in 1945 of *This Other Planet*, 'the best war poetry in the correct sense of the term that I have seen in these past six years.'

His *Collected Poems* were published in 2001 by David Philip in Cape Town and James Currey in Oxford. It includes 'The Africa We Knew', 'Tiresias', 'This Other Planet', 'Indian Landscape', 'Between Two Worlds', 'Formal Spring' and 'Flashback to America'.

FAMILIES

Stella Martin Currey: playwright and novelist

Stella Martin Currey was apprenticed at the age of 19 as a reporter on the Bristol *Evening Times & Echo*. She was given a pioneering women's page, 'Apples of Eve', and started a diary as if it were being written by the animals in Clifton Zoo. Her first novel, *Paperchase End*, was about the renowned Bristol newspaper war between rival owners in 1929/30. In *Rebel Women Between the Wars* (2024), Sarah Lonsdale picked her out as one of a cluster of rebellious women journalists establishing themselves after the First World War in a tough profession run by men. When married, she was successful at getting her short stories into London magazines and occasionally into high paying journals in the United States. The income she earned from her writing paid for her sons to go to boarding school at Kingswood in Bath. Persephone Press recently republished *One Woman's Year* (1952) in its elegant grey format. In the 1950s she turned to the much more demanding medium of theatre and the Colchester Repertory Theatre commissioned her plays from her to start each season. Her agent was on the edge of getting West End performances of her plays into London theatres. She wrote a play for the new medium of television about the family pressures on a working-class girl of getting a scholarship to a high school through the eleven-plus examination. Stella and Ralph in 1934 encouraged J. P. Martin, to write down the stories he told about Uncle the elephant who wears a purple dressing gown and rides in a traction engine. It took them until 1960, drawing on all their London publishing contacts, to get Jonathan Cape, the publishers of the renowned Arthur Ransome books, to accept J. P. Martin's six *Uncle* books.

I felt intimidated by my father's skill with the craft of poetry, so did not attempt to write poetry myself. My brother Andrew John Colborne Currey, however, did have some success with placing poems in established journals such as the TLS. I was born into a family of writers, so was considered to have gone over to the other side when I joined Oxford University Press.

Family Tree

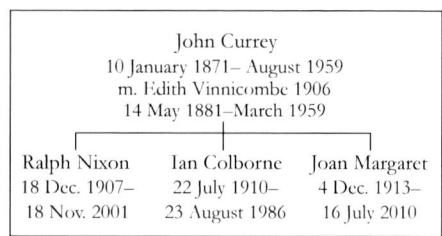

John Currey
10 January 1871– August 1959
m. Edith Vinnicombe 1906
14 May 1881–March 1959

Ralph Nixon	Ian Colborne	Joan Margaret
18 Dec. 1907–	22 July 1910–	4 Dec. 1913–
18 Nov. 2001	23 August 1986	16 July 2010

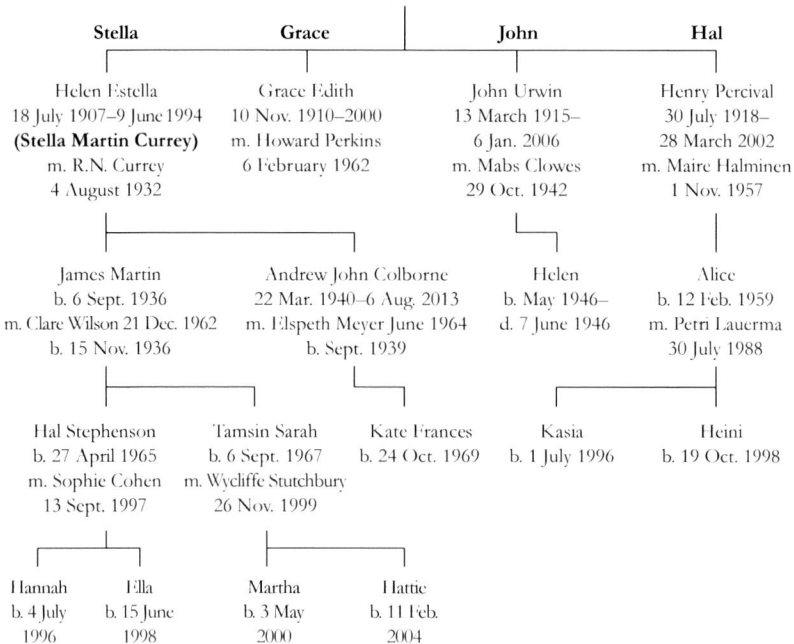

Percy
John Percival
5 Aug. 1879–24 March 1966
J.P. Martin (JPM)
m. **Nancy** Annie Mann, 19 Oct. 1906
d. 15 February 1944
m. **Jane** Jenny Sowerbutts
(née Mann) 31 Dec. 1947

Stella	**Grace**	**John**	**Hal**
Helen Estella	Grace Edith	John Urwin	Henry Percival
18 July 1907–9 June 1994	10 Nov. 1910–2000	13 March 1915–	30 July 1918–
(Stella Martin Currey)	m. Howard Perkins	6 Jan. 2006	28 March 2002
m. R.N. Currey	6 February 1962	m. Mabs Clowes	m. Maire Halminen
4 August 1932		29 Oct. 1942	1 Nov. 1957

James Martin	Andrew John Colborne	Helen	Alice
b. 6 Sept. 1936	22 Mar. 1940–6 Aug. 2013	b. May 1946–	b. 12 Feb. 1959
m. Clare Wilson 21 Dec. 1962	m. Elspeth Meyer June 1964	d. 7 June 1946	m. Petri Lauerma
b. 15 Nov. 1936	b. Sept. 1939		30 July 1988

Hal Stephenson	Tamsin Sarah	Kate Frances	Kasia	Heini
b. 27 April 1965	b. 6 Sept. 1967	b. 24 Oct. 1969	b. 1 July 1996	b. 19 Oct. 1998
m. Sophie Cohen	m. Wycliffe Stutchbury			
13 Sept. 1997	26 Nov. 1999			

Hannah	Ella	Martha	Hattie
b. 4 July 1996	b. 15 June 1998	b. 3 May 2000	b. 11 Feb. 2004

ONE
All the Fun of a War

Beverley Road, Colchester

In 1936, after I was born, my parents Ralph and Stella moved into a Victorian terraced house at 3 Beverley Road, Colchester; after the war they were paying £75 a year in rent, so reluctantly bought the house for £1500 pounds. They lived there until Stella died in 1994 and Ralph in 2002. In other words, it was the house I always had as my family base until I was 67. Hannah and Ella remember visiting their great-grandfather there and being given 'sweeties'. Ralph had a chance to admire Martha but Hattie arrived a bit too late to meet him. After his death, Ronald Blythe and I arranged a meeting of readings of his poetry in the big hall at the Colchester Royal Grammar School, which was only five minutes' walk away. Following that there was a party on the front steps of his home, which Hannah and Ella enjoyed so much that one of them asked Clare when she was going to have a funeral party.

Roman soldier at bottom of garden

The following photograph is of me standing on Stella's knees examining a Penguin book on the stony beach at Aldeburgh on the Suffolk coast. Clearly, a suitable picture of someone destined to publish the Penguins of Africa, the African Writers Series.

I can identify my first memory as being in February 1939 when I was about two and a half years' old. In Pietermaritzburg in 1960, I could still accurately describe to my father's cousin Freda Wood the dormer window of the house in which she had been packing

ALL THE FUN OF A WAR

Stella with James on the beach at Aldeburgh in Suffolk in 1937, examining one of the first Penguin Books, which were launched that year.

her trunk to sail to South Africa before the outbreak of war. There is a picture of me, with blonde curly hair, clambering on a pile of earth above the opening of a deep trench; this was in the summer of 1939 when Ralph and his archaeologist schoolmaster colleague, A. F. Hall, were digging down to prove that the edge of the Roman road from Colchester to London went under the back garden of 3 Beverley Road.

A. F. Hall had drawn a line from the Britanno-Roman ramparts to the Balkerne Gate in the Roman wall. He was right about that because they found a Roman soldier buried eight feet down with a penny in his mouth to pay for his ferry across the River Styx. The Romans buried their dead on the edge of highways where they left the cities. This soldier had been left to lie there until that day, and I remember the trench and the excitement.

During the Second World War the Roman ramparts were deepened to provide tank traps, which were wonderful for cycling and skidding. Over the wall, where earth was being dug out to build car garages, the centurion Longinus's tombstone was found and was displayed prominently in the Colchester Castle museum.

Stella doted on my curly hair and brilliant blue eyes. Women have remarked on my bright blue eyes throughout my life. Clare remembered them on being first introduced to me by George Cacanas in Oxford when I was wearing a pale blue woollen tie.

Cakes in Belgium ready for Babar

My first substantial memories are attached to a seaside holiday in Belgium in August 1939. I remember cake shops with rows of cakes like a picture in Babar the Baby Elephant. I remember running frightened down a heavily carpeted corridor to find my Aunt Joan who was baby-sitting me. I remember the lighthouse outside the hotel window at breakfast. I remember a canal boat trip to Bruges.

What I did not know was that Ralph and Stella had been determined to take the holiday and that the family got back by ferry only three weeks before the start of the Second World War against Germany on 3 September 1939.

On my third birthday on 6 September 1939, a large box was sent by Aunt Joan from Footman's Store in Ipswich and out of it, on a sunny day in the back garden of 3 Beverley Road Colchester, came the teddy bear that still sits on the windowsill at Walkern Mill. Within days the blue skies above Colchester would be criss-crossed with the vapour trails of the Battle of Britain.

All the fun of a war

My memories of the start of the war are of all sorts of diverting happenings, but I have no memory of worry. I was much taken with my Mickey Mouse gas mask with its wobbling nose. I 'helped' stick tape across the window panes to stop splinters of glass should there be a bomb. Black blinds were being put up. Ralph gas-proofed the basement where a bomb shelter, like a large steel table containing a double bed was being assembled, and to which the family would descend when the air-raid warning siren sounded. There was much collecting and storing of the fruits of the autumn, as well as much bottling and stacking of shining Kilner Jars in the basement pantry, where eggs were preserved in bowls of waterglass. I liked winding the machine that shredded runner beans.

Number 3 Beverley Road is a four-storey Victorian brick terrace house built in about 1860. On the top floor were to be bedrooms for me and my brother Andrew and a box room where, as we grew older, we would build model towns out of blocks and dinky toys. On the first floor Ralph and Stella's bedroom faced the street and, at the back, the nursery overlooked the garden with its apple, pear and laburnum trees. On the ground floor there was a double doorway arch between the sitting and dining rooms, which was good for acting in plays and playing charades; since the two rooms ran from east to west it meant that the evening light shone through to the dining room and the morning light lit up the living room with its wall of bookcases. The kitchen was a separate single-storey building with a roof over which Andrew and I could later climb into the window of the lavatory. The basement was a utility area and it became a play area for our young friends who were pleased to climb in through the front window; there was a notice to the gang of boys signed 'By Order Chief', who was me. But that was after the war.

Shandy Colchester Cromwell

At the age of three I was afraid of dogs, so for Christmas 1939 I was given a brown and white fox terrier puppy named Shandy Colchester Cromwell. The two of us became friends within 15 minutes and remained so for the next 14 years. In the black-out Shandy was hit by a car and carried home unconscious by Ralph. I remember Shandy being visited by the vet and slowly recovering in a basket in front of the gas fire in the dining room.

On 22 March 1940 Andrew was born and my great aunt Jane came to housekeep. I had a beautiful whistle painted in shiny rings of brightly coloured paint. Aunt Jane confiscated it because she said it was disturbing my mother. I did not blame Andrew or my mother Stella, but remember my delight at finding it after the war and my fury with fierce Aunt Jane.

During the summer of 1940 Stella, Ralph, Andrew and I were in Colchester. As the town was near the east coast it would be in the front line of invasion. It did not suffer bombing because, on 16 July 1940 after the fall of France, Hitler's generals had, in Operation Sea Lion, planned to seize the Colchester garrison more or less intact as a base from which to divide England diagonally in half and establish a capital at Oxford.

On 15 September 1940, the mothers of young children in Colchester were told, at only three hours' notice, to catch a train provided for evacuees to Liverpool Street station in London. The station had been bombed the night before and I remember the excitement of crossing fire hoses and crunching glass to climb up into my uncle Tom Currey's gigantic yellow American Studebaker limousine complete with a driver in a cap who drove us to Aunt Sally and Uncle Tom's house at Rickmansworth on the northern edge of London.

While drinking cups of tea on the lawn beside the tennis court, everybody could see vapour trails from the German and British fighters crisscrossing the skies while shooting one another down in the Battle of Britain. After the war, we learnt that the Luftwaffe's failure that weekend to establish air supremacy in that battle meant that only two days later, on 17 September 1940, Hitler called off Operation Sea Lion as a means of invading Britain.

After that the Germans decided to 'blitz' Britain's cities with air raids that would kill many people, including children. The civilian casualties for the first two years were worse than those in the armed services. The Nazis expected to break the morale of ordinary British people with bombing and then invading at a later date.

Refugees to the centre of England

The Currey family was evacuated to Daventry right in the centre of England where great radio masts broadcast to the empire and occupied Europe with the call sign of 'Daventry Calling! Daventry Calling!' Stella's father J. P. Martin, author of the Uncle series of children's stories, was the Methodist minister. Mine and Andrew's grandmother was called Nancy and she had recently had a serious operation, so the house was run by the maid Kate Bell.

J. P. Martin wrote on 16 September 1940 that there are 'hundreds of refugees in this small town and district and now my own family join them. Stella, Ralph, James and Andrew – Andrew lying in a Moses basket – arrived here.'

My (James's) adopted cousin from Czechoslovakia had been sent away on a Kindertransport with his name on a label round his wrist and without his mother. My daughter-in-law Sophie's father, Bernard Cohen, had gone from the London East End and on the first morning could not make out what were all these woolly blobs on green; it was the first time he had seen fields and sheep.

J. P. Martin took the ways of children for granted. As a Methodist minister he worked at home for most of the week from his study in the great big brick manse and did not mind if Andrew, Shandy and I were there. I always felt, when I was with my other grandfather John Currey, that I might get things wrong. However, I found my South African grandmother Edith gentle and interested in telling me stories about her childhood growing up on farms in South Africa; Andrew and I did not see much of them as they were in Sevenoaks, south of London and not far from the worst bombing.

Signals training in the soot-black north

Ralph Currey was called up for National Service in the armed forces and in the winter of 1941 was sent for training in the Royal Signals on the moors around the soot-black northern mill town of Huddersfield. To be near him Stella rented some grubby rooms called 'digs'. There was a public park with a gloomy pond nearby into which Andrew fell. I picture repeatedly passing a shop window in which there were good strong wooden toys and an army lorry, which was given to me at Christmas. In a bookshop I remember Stella showing me a Van Gogh painting of crows over a yellow wheatfield.

The biggest treat was that often the family trundled off for Sunday lunch in a little steam train to Holmfirth, where Ralph had become friends with Dr Bryan and Jenny Meyer. Their daughter was called Elspeth. One Sunday, despite many adult warnings, I fell off a snowy wall in their steep garden and dislodged a boulder, which nearly fell on Elspeth. I was in big trouble. I woke up in the night with pain from my bruises but when Stella took me to the big bright hygienic doctor's bathroom, she fiercely told me that it served me right.

Malcolm Ford, the art master at CRGS, was also posted near Holmfirth and recalled being invited out to tea and finding a tiger looking out of the front window. The tiger had later lain down in front of an alderman's funeral procession and had to go to a zoo.

Stella got the publishing firm Thomas Nelson to commission scraper board engravings from Malcolm Ford for each of the 12 months in *One Woman's Year*, first published in 1983 and still selling more than forty years later. Royalties come yearly from Persephone Press in Bath.

In 1964, Elspeth Meyer was to marry my brother Andrew. Both Elspeth and I remembered the treat at the railway station when, as a steam engine was being shunted to the back of the train to return to Huddersfield, the driver who heaved coals from the tender into the glowing boiler allowed us to ride on the footplate. While the family was in Huddersfield, Shandy the dog used to send letters to me and Andrew, which he got Granny Nancy to post:

> When I passed the baker's dog the other day he growled 'evacuee!' How can this be when I'm adopted – properly – by the Martin family till you get back. This morning I was just coming back from a walk when an Alsatian – a giant dog – turned the corner and growled, 'where do you live?' I barked, 'at Kingsthorpe with Mr and Mrs Martin.' He barked back, 'Quite respectable. Pass on Macduff.' Why I don't know!

Stella's most successful book of the war was called *Following Charles*, which was in the form of a diary about a young mother moving with children to where her husband was posted. It was reprinted several times.

Daventry calling! Daventry calling!

In May 1942 Stella, Andrew and I returned to Daventry. We had to change trains at the great steel and cutlery town of Sheffield and I remember the fun of crunching through broken glass along the bombed platform. Ralph then went into the Royal Artillery to work with radar, the magical new invention that could detect bombers and fighters out of sight behind the bend of the earth; he served at various anti-aircraft gun sites on the Kent coast facing Belgium and France and occasionally came back on leave. The first radar trial had taken place just before the war from BBC masts and a Handley Page bomber was detected flying over Daventry.

In June 1943 Ralph set sail for India and his family did not see him again until 1946. In passing through South Africa he left a cheque at the big Stuttafords store in Cape Town and it was always an exciting event when the grey fibre boxes were opened and out came crystallised fruit or Cape gooseberry jam. His letters included his rather good drawings of animals, people and basha bamboo huts. The pictures were small and neat because they had been reduced photographically to save weight on the airmail plane. I, with so much other adult attention, do not remember missing Ralph a great deal.

There was very little traffic so, morning and afternoon, I could walk without a grown-up to and from Miss Wilfrid's 'dame school' next to the Methodist chapel. I tried my hardest and took to reading. I liked the picture of fruit and vegetables in a greengrocer's shop in the maths book for calculating sums in the immensely complicated pounds, shillings and pence. However, I felt that Miss Wilfrid favoured the girls and I was annoyed that, for the war effort, we were told to use only one sheet of toilet paper in the lavatory.

On the way to school there were changing coloured posters outside the Regal Cinema advertising films like *Gone With the Wind* and Walt Disney's *Bambi* and *Dumbo*. The best film was Shakespeare's *Henry V* featuring clouds of arrows falling heroically on the French; the important thing was that, like a football match, England won.

The engineers from the BBC radio station on the hill would put on a pantomime in the Regal and one year they made a mechanical owl, which thrilled me and Andrew, and our elders, by flying across the stage with its wings flapping. Opposite the cinema was the police station with an unchanging permanent coloured photograph to warn people about the Colorado beetle among their potatoes. There were so few coloured things in war time that I used often to look at this unchanging poster. From the immensely tall masts on the hill above Daventry the BBC Empire Service went out across the world to encourage the Australians and Canadians and Indians who were on our side against the Nazis – I liked calling them 'the Nasties'. 'Daventry Calling! Daventry Calling!' went ringing round the world.

The wonder of a bike

The small group of boys at school was dominated by a farmer's son called John Thomas who was a magical liar. He cut black and white pictures of highly-priced stamps out of a stamp catalogue, insisted they were genuine and persuaded the other boys to buy them although they sort of knew they were fake. He took the boys to a field below 'the rec' (recreation ground) and pointed to a shed in the middle of a field. John Thomas said that he had taken a black model of a bomber, rubbed it with bicycle oil and that it had grown and was in that shed. The other boys jumped up and down with excitement and said they wanted to see it but he said that they would be arrested if they climbed over the padlocked gate.

Matthew Moser, the doctor's son, was my best friend, and he lived just down on the other side of Badby Road, had many of the enviable toys of a more prosperous family and also a large garden and a pigeon loft. Someone asked whether Dr Moser was a 'Jew'. I did not know what a 'Jew' was.

I was devoted to a battered child-sized bike, which my Uncle Ian had got for me with great difficulty, as no children's bikes were being made at that time. To begin with, I could only mount it by leaning against a wall or tree. On one occasion I fell off in a country lane and only had banks of nettles against which somehow to get back onto it.

The bike also allowed me to cycle about three miles out of town on the Staverton road, near the Thomas's farm, to have pony riding lessons. On the way, I would be excited when I came across unexpected events like the great orange red box of a threshing machine with a traction engine supplying power along a spinning belt while men with pitchforks heaved sheaves of wheat into the top, and the grain shot out into 200-pound hessian sacks. These were the days before combine harvesters became common; indeed, there were hardly any tractors.

In summer, the fresh smell of hot tar might come wafting round a bend as gravel was being scattered and rolled by a steam roller. In a vacant lot opposite the manse was a steam shovel called a Ruston-Bucyrus, which sounds like the name of an historic monster. Nearby, an engineering factory burnt down, attracting an exciting number of fire engines, and my friends and I watched the site smouldering for days later. The most dramatic Christmas was when the water pumping station burnt down and everybody had to fetch their water in buckets from water carts in the streets.

Inventing games

Grandpa Martin was devoted to Christmas. He would spend time in the cellar with me and Andrew carving faces out of logs to burn on the fire so that flames leapt out of the mouth and eyes. There were lots of games and charades. Many of the games such as Alsatia, Spider and Markets had been invented by J. P. Martin himself. He felt slightly guilty about his game called Christmas Card Snap. Being a Methodist parson, practically all the cards he received were hideous. After Christmas, the cards would be dealt out to the players round the table and the one voted the ugliest was the winner of that round. J. P. Martin would get me to help him paste – with paste made out of flour and water – his newspaper cuttings about the way the war was proceeding. I liked copying the maps, especially the one of Libya, which had straight boundaries. I took a great interest in the liberal *News Chronicle* for practising my reading.

Andrew and I would visit Granny Nancy for 'titbits' because she was having breakfast in bed every day. She was fragile after an operation and sometimes could not even get downstairs for teatime. Nancy, Stella and Kate were very interested in a big house auction sale on 18 February 1944. Matthew Moser said that his mother would be bidding at it for two horses and I hoped I might be able to ride them. He then told me that his mother had made the highest bid, and I was most excited when he took me back to his home to see them. There they were: two rearing metal statues on the mantelpiece. I was desperately disappointed and went back up the Badby Road to the manse.

Unexpectedly, my mother Stella came out onto the front steps and told me how she had taken Granny to that house sale, but that after they got home she died. I now sadly think that I was more upset about the Moser horses. When Uncle John, who worked in RAF bomb disposal was on compassionate leave, I wanted to show him something from the drawing room, but was shocked to find Granny Nancy lying in a coffin. I crept out saying nothing.

I introduce the cake queue to the Gaderene swine

People at the chapel took it for granted that children of the manse would know the hymns and Bible stories, but nothing could have been further from the truth. I came nearest to demonstrating that I was being brought up as expected while out Christmas shopping one year in Leamington Spa. Stella had already collected a copy of *The Children's Bible*, which she had ordered from a bookseller as one of my presents. She then asked me to keep her place in a cake queue while she went to another shop, but when she came back she found me reading the story of the Gadarene swine aloud to the cake queue. On the train afterwards, I told Stella that I had never heard the story before but found it interesting, 'as did the queue', I added firmly.

As a Methodist minister, Sunday was *the* big working day for J. P. Martin. Since he worked from home for most of the week, activities with his grandsons provided him with easy breaks from the administration of his circuit. The door of his study at the end of a long upstairs passage was never closed to me, Andrew or Shandy. Many a sermon was prepared with Shandy asleep by the gas fire and Andrew in the shadowy kneehole of the desk drawing or building a town or farmyard.

On coming back from school one afternoon, and being met as usual by Shandy running rapturously down the stairs from the study, I shouted, 'Shandy's pink! All his white is pink!' JPM and Andrew had been happily engaged in touching up the threadbare patches of the shabby red carpet in the study with red ink, and Shandy had rolled in it. Grandpa taught me a certain amount of gardening and I was so delighted with the reception given to my first harvest of carrots that I shouted at the table, 'Let's have another lovely carrot lunch from my garden on my birthday!'

To steal! To forge!

One Sunday, I cycled out with JPM to an afternoon service at Naseby, which was where one of the most famous battles in the civil war had been fought. On our return, JPM gave me the collection to count and I slipped a couple of sixpences aside for myself. When Stella came in to see me in bed, she asked me if I had kept some of the money. She told me that my grandfather was not cross, did not believe I had stolen it, and that he himself must have made a mistake. She also told me that if I owned up my grandfather would forgive me. I agreed with relief and Stella talked through with me what was meant by 'stealing'. At another time, I was not practising much between my piano lessons, so the teacher drew a box in the back of my exercise book containing the days of the week so that Stella could initial it each day after I had practised. I still failed to practise and thought that I could easily replicate her initials instead. The teacher then told Stella who had to explain to me what 'forgery' meant.

Andrew and I found a firm friend in Kate Bell. She was queen of the huge old-fashioned kitchen with its glowing coal range on which she cooked for us. I, who was fond of exercising my new skill, would read her favourite poems aloud to her while she was ironing or cleaning the silver. We boys used her kitchen table to make railways or paste up big pictures of our grandparents' house.

Andrew and I were always excited when Aunt Grace came to visit us from Bristol because her suitcase was always full of presents. She worked as a nurse in Bristol and one night had been blown under a patient's bed by the blast of a bomb. A couple of times, Stella took Andrew and me for a holiday via Bristol where Aunt Grace would give us treats before we went on to the seaside resort of Clevedon with its Victorian pier.

Down the coast at Weston-Super-Mare, we would stay with our South African cousin Freda Wood, who had two children, Graham and Heather, and an adopted son Ralph. At that time, her husband Lieutenant-Colonel Cecil Wood was away fighting the Germans and Italians in North Africa.

In the summer of 1939, under a scheme organised by Sir Nicholas Winton, the Woods had collected a Jewish refugee boy from Liverpool Street station in London. He was one of the 669 Kindertransport children arriving by boat and train from Prague in Czechoslovakia, which had just been invaded by the Nazis. Freda and Cecil were handed Ralph aged three who had a label round his neck and a neatly packed suitcase in which his mother, who expected to be sent to Auschwitz with her husband, had put presents for his next three birthdays and had folded bigger and bigger new clothes. I adored Ralph because he was so naughty and together we did horrid things to my well-behaved cousins Graham and Heather.

They are waiting to go to the 'second front'

Andrew and I liked our grandfather JPM's brother Uncle Norman, who worked in a big office in London advertising furniture. He would take walks with his neatly furled umbrella and say, 'I think it is going to rain', then put up his umbrella and spray the path with pennies for the boys to pick up and keep. Andrew and I were later told that he had helped organise the escapes of Jews to Britain from Austria and Germany.

In the spring of 1944, all the adults were talking about when the United States, Britain and the Commonwealth countries would open 'the second front' on the beaches of western Europe. I knew from maps and pictures in the *News Chronicle* that the Russians were fighting the Germans in giant tank battles led by Marshall Zhukov. J. P. Martin was anxious to know from his brother Norman what the businessmen in the City of London were saying about the date when 'the second front' would open.

In St James's Street, opposite Matthew Moser's house in Daventry, there had been an army encampment for weeks, and Matthew and I spent our afternoons talking to the soldiers as they waterproofed the engines of their trucks, jeeps and guns. I told my great-uncle Norman that 'they are waiting to go to the second front.' 'Then they've got a long wait,' Uncle Norman replied. 'Everybody in the City says it can't possibly happen for a couple of weeks.' When I set off for school that Monday St James's Street was empty. At lunch I announced that 'the second front will open tomorrow. All the lorries have gone from St James's Street.'

On Tuesday 6 June 1944 I thought I would be told off for being late for lunch because I had been watching a man mend his merry-go-round at the funfair, which had arrived at the 'rec'. I came back to be cheered by the family with a chorus of cries of 'it's D-Day!' I had got it right and Uncle Norman had got it wrong. Distracting rumours of a later date had been spread round the City.

JPM and I pasted into a scrapbook the exciting newspaper cuttings from Normandy as the Allies advanced, sweeping round Paris. JPM knew that Uncle John was in this great advance somewhere in Belgium in October where he was delousing the very hotel at Knokke in which we had stayed in 1939.

After the war, John told Stella that in bomb disposal you were in a mental duel with the German who had laid a trail of tripwires and bombs. John and his RAF team went on defusing bombs and mines on airfields in Germany in February 1945. He later received the British Empire Medal for his meticulous work day after day as his colleagues were being blown up in front of his eyes. Soon after the war my mother went off without warning because John wanted to talk to her about the awful realities of his work. In September 1944, she had brought a tall young man who belonged to the Methodist chapel into our bedroom. He was in his paratrooper's uniform and his maroon beret seemed almost to hit the ceiling.

A day or two later, on 17 September 1944, we watched endless planes towing gliders flying above the manse. A few hours later we all rushed out to see the bombers coming back in their hundreds, with towing ropes trailing behind them. This was after they had landed the paratroopers for what turned out to be the bitter Battle of Arnhem (featured in *A Bridge Too Far*) across the Rhine into Germany. The move was too bold, but if it had worked it would have shortened the war. Many of the paratroopers were killed, including the handsome young man who came into our room.

Mumps! This Christmas's fashionable disease

That bedroom sticks in my memory. Footsteps rose from the street and, if it was raining, I would feel glad to be warm in bed. There was a tall wardrobe in it with a door into which Andrew and I would climb as if into a coach. It wobbled but never fell over. Soon after Christmas each year, Andrew and I would both fall ill with whatever happened to be that year's fashionable infectious disease – whooping cough, measles, mumps, though never rubella, which was luridly called scarlet fever. These are now prevented by the MMR vaccine. Each year I was given another Arthur Ransome book for Christmas and another one during my illness.

In January 1944, I was extremely ill with mumps and, it later turned out, had a rare complication that left me stone deaf in my right ear. I sort of realised I was not hearing in one ear but, aged about eight, never mentioned it to any adults either at home or school. It did not bother me, so I did not bother them. I perhaps realised there would be a terrible fuss – which there was a couple of years later.

In January 1945 there was no prospect of Ralph returning from India in the foreseeable future, as the war against Japan continued relentlessly. There was hope of the war ending with Germany and so it was decided that it would be safe enough for Stella, Andrew and me to go back to Colchester near the east coast. Air raids had stopped, although V-1 unmanned flying bombs, 'doodlebugs', were still being dropped randomly on the eastern counties and London. While sitting outside on the front steps, I heard one flying over Beverley Road sounding like a motorbike; children at school were trained that if the noise stopped they must rush for a shelter or lie behind a wall.

Royal purple and a queen

I had to start at the preparatory school – 'the pree' as it was pronounced – for Colchester Royal Grammar School because of the introduction of what came to be called 'the eleven-plus exam'. This followed Butler's 1944 Education Act, which enabled the best pupils to be selected to go free to the grammar school. Unfortunately, I was the only new boy starting in the second term. The school was 'royal' so, because of 'Henry VIII and Elizabeth I and all our benefactors', the boys wore purple uniforms. The purple cap was late in arriving so Stella sent me to the 'pre' in the red cap of my Daventry school for which I was miserably teased and bullied.

I remember the sirens sounding, going to the shelters in the grounds round the school and us all singing together while sitting on forms (benches with wooden tops and metal legs.)

The new neighbours at 4 Beverley Road were the Johnsons; Leonie Johnson's husband had been a regular army officer who was killed in North Africa during the war. Judith and I were more or less of an age, as were Andrew and Jonathan. They first came round to try and catch a mouse in our kitchen. We became firm friends, climbed over one another's garden fences and played in Beverley Road as there were no cars. We helped one another out as rationing became worse after the war when the food that had reached us from the United States during the war, was being diverted to starving Europe. Bread and potatoes went on ration and even coal in the severely cold winter of 1947.

In May 1945 everybody was expecting the war in Europe to end and, on 8 May, when the news came through, our teacher Miss Stanyon sent us home early. I got French, American and Russian flags to hang by the road, and was upset when a passerby stole, or objected to, the bright red Russian flag with its hammer and sickle.

Stella, Andrew and I spent the August school holidays with her father, J. P. Martin, at Daventry. As I was waking up in the room above the porch one morning, with bright sunlight coming in through the red curtains, Stella came in with something important to say. She told me that the extraordinarily powerful atom bomb had been dropped in Japan and that this would perhaps shorten the war and mean that Daddy might be coming home earlier. V-J Day was 15 August 1945 and was not as much fun as V-E Day had been. All I remember was a corpulent man doing belly flops from the top board at Clevedon swimming pool.

Stone deaf in my right ear

It was another six months before, on 28 March 1946, Andrew and I watched Ralph's much anticipated arrival in a taxi through the bay windows of 3 Beverley Road. It had taken him three days to fly from Bombay knee-to-knee in the windowless bomb-bay of a Liberator bomber. They had stopped many times and at Haifa he had got our family a whole basket of oranges, which he was carrying up the front path.

Stella's brother Uncle Hal was demobilised from Palestine on the same day as Ralph was from India and they spoke on the telephone for the first time in three years. Ralph then put the phone receiver into my right hand, but I insisted, with quite a tussle, on switching it to my left hand so that I could speak to my uncle. After the call, Ralph and Stella wanted to know why I had switched the phone to my left ear.

Why had I not told Stella that I could not hear in my right ear? All I remember is that I had noticed but it had not bothered me. Nobody had noticed. I was made to feel naughty, as if I had concealed a secret. There followed doctors, specialists, clinics, fuss. There was no hope that there could be an operation. It was a rare complication from the mumps I had suffered soon after Christmas. Since I could only have mumps once, my left ear would not be affected in the same way. My left ear maintained its ability to respond to high frequencies and I could hear the high-pitched squeak of bats well into adulthood. Apparently, if I had suffered the complication in my teens it could have affected my fertility.

The return of Ralph from India is rather a let-down

There had been a tremendous build up to my father Ralph's return, and there were exciting times like unpacking his boxes and trunks. I was paid a penny a pair for polishing some twenty pairs of shoes. A kukri knife, and ornaments such as a marble decorative carving (as on the Taj Mahal), degchi saucepans and spices and instructions from his bearer servant for cooking curry, which was then hardly known in Britain. (Nowadays it is suggested that it has replaced roast beef as the English national dish.) I disliked being nicknamed 'Hot Stuff'. It turned out later that at his grammar school my father had been called 'Killer Currey' because of his hot, temper. Ralph had brought me and Andrew Indian cricket bats which our mates scorned for being inferior to English ones; Ralph, Andrew, Jon from next door and I played cricket with a tennis ball in the back garden. I found, however, without quite recognising what had changed, that Ralph's return was a bit of a let-down. He told me off much more than Stella, who had been looking after me for some five years, ever did. I now had a rival for my mother's attention and this put me out without me quite understanding why.

My uncle Hal Martin often used to come and stay with us during and after the war and it was he who introduced me and Andrew to classical music, art and later the excitements of travelling in Europe. While Hal himself was still at school in 1938, he became a real enthusiast for European languages. Mr Barnes, the teacher of French and German at Kingswood School in Bath, arranged for a dozen boys to go on an exchange visit to Ifeld, one of the most elite National Socialist schools in Germany. They had to wear Nazi uniforms and take part in all the ferocious physical exercises and competitions. A party of German boys had then paid a return visit to Kingswood and what Hal Martin remembered most about it was that the son of the German ambassador, Joachim von Ribbentrop, kept on letting down the deckchairs of the people watching the British tribal ritual of cricket.

After my father's return from India in the summer of 1946, for our first family holiday my father and mother chose Knaplock Farm on Exmoor, which was approximately a mile above Tarr Steps, a prehistoric bridge constructed from slabs of granite. My parents had ordered Arthur Ransome's *Great Northern* for my birthday on 6 September 1946, so the poor postman, who had no van, had to do his daily round of the moor on foot and, to get to us had to carry the book across those dramatic stones.

It was harvest time and I went to watch the reaper. Stella came up to collect me for lunch and, as she approached the gate, the farmer's 14-year-old son came tearing down past her. She cried out to him but he rushed past saying nothing. Stella thought something had happened to me. She found me deeply shocked looking at where the reaper had cut off the legs of the farm fox terrier we all loved. Soon afterwards, when J. P. Martin and Aunt Jane moved to Timberscombe, which is near Dunster with Dunkery Beacon to the west, we always went on holiday in the West Country.

The frozen winter of 1947

When I started at the 'pre' I came twenty-third in class and thought that, because it was a high number, I was doing well. I was coming across new subjects like geography, which taught me about a wider world. I was already interested in maps. I climbed up the class but Andrew Hamer was always top. One week Ralph gave me a florin (10p) because Miss Stanyon had been pleased to tell Ralph that, for once, I was top of the class. However, James suspected it was only because he had cheated in a spelling test by changing the word 'business' – at least he learnt how to spell the word. Ralph told me that people like Andrew Hamer peaked at the level of the School Certificate (now called GCSE), but did not go to the sixth form and university. It was quite difficult having a father as a master; when Ralph had to go into Miss Stanyon's class one day, Andrew lifted the lid of his desk and hid his head in it.

School breaks were important times of the day, with the bomb shelters used for all sorts of games like hide and seek. Every now and again everybody would decide to play at being archaeologists and set about digging into the banks of the shelters. Given that Colchester had been the Romans' first capital in England, the boys actually found Roman pottery – what stood out most was the broken orange Samian ware imported from Belgium almost two thousand years earlier. Boys were always boasting about finding coins, but I was never actually shown one. One boy claimed to have tried to use a Roman coin to pay his fare on one of the corporation buses run by Colchester Town Council – their maroon colour introduced some brightness to the wartime streets.

The boys had one accent in school but resorted to their broad Essex one in the playground and outside school; 'gena ketch a corpo' meant 'I am going to catch a corporation bus.' Stella was always correcting our Essex accents. The year 1947 had one of the two worst winters in the second half of the twentieth century. I remember the awful pain of my fingers coming back to life after my woollen gloves had become sodden from snowballing or sliding down the slopes of the shelters. When the thaw suddenly came, the grounds between the shelters would flood and boys in Wellington boots would float upside-down benches as motorboats.

Trading Beano *and* Dandy

There was much trading in the breaks. Ralph and Stella refused to buy me or Andrew the *Beano* and *Dandy* comics that cost twopence. The boys whose parents had bought them copies would sell them for a penny and, since I could sell them on for a penny, they cost me nothing. Dinky Toys were also much traded. None had been made during the war and the paint had chipped off the pre-war ones. Andrew and I were delighted one Sunday before Christmas when, for the first time since the war, we saw bright sparkling new Dinky Toys in the window of the West End Bicycle Shop. Stella went to queue early on Monday morning and was allowed to buy one Dinky each for Andrew and me. A year or two later, I shoplifted a maroon Oldsmobile saloon car and, though not caught, was frightened enough not to try it again.

Ice cream vans came to the school grounds and their cornets cost threepence; I once borrowed sixpence from somebody called Howard to buy my first ever choc-ice and am still ashamed that I did not get round to paying back the loan.

An immensely successful toy was metal Meccano from which one bolted together lorries and huts; the picture on the front of the box was of Tower Bridge in London made from Meccano; it was a lingering disappointment that nothing like that could be built with the handful of pieces supplied in the box. With the encouragement of my South African grandmother, I had become interested in stamp collecting and was given a Whitfield King & Co. of Ipswich catalogue in compensation for a distressing examination of my deaf ear involving a specialist putting noisy things into my ears.

In Crouch Street and the library

Ralph and Stella were living in a flat in Crouch Street Colchester at the time of my birth in 1936. Stella continued to use the Crouch Street food shops after the war. At Wrights the grocers, she would be given a chair to sit on while she 'gave the order' for delivery. A male shop assistant in brown overalls would funnel loose sugar, rice and grains into brown and blue paper bags on scales with weights. It took a long time but there were lots of other things for me to look at and wish to be able to eat. Stella did not pay before leaving the shop as the bills were always put on the account, which was paid by cheque on the last delivery of the month.

The smell of roasting coffee poured out into the street from Guntons. At that time Mr Gunton was considered too expensive, but he later took over our supplies for Beverley Road. A few doors along was Frank Wright the butcher, where great carcasses of beef or lamb were carved up on wooden benches that had worn into beautiful rounded shapes; Mrs Wright took payment at the till behind a sash window.

Hearsums, the fishmonger, had coloured tile pictures of fishermen catching fish at sea and farmers shooting pheasants. There was a great marble slab in the centre, which was open to the street to disperse the fishy smells.

When the groceries were delivered I used to check them out of the box against the bill before Stella put them in the cupboards. I enjoyed unpacking Stella's shopping and asked what was in one packet. She answered, 'you know I will always tell you the truth.

Daddy and I have you and we have Andrew. We love you both but we do not think that we want to have any more brothers or sisters and this is to stop that happening.'

I was soon trusted to go into town on my own and was given jobs to do, often in the enormous post office. On Saturday mornings I would meet friends and we would look enviously in the windows of Sands toy shop at the Hornby model railways my parents would never buy for us. There was one bookshop called Shippeys and another run by Mr Griggs. He unfortunately had had a fire and, although he had a far better range of books, they tended to be a little grubby.

In the town centre was the handsome neo-Georgian library with enormous glittering sash windows. By then the strips of brown tape had been taken off and the food office for issuing ration books had closed. I used to spend hours choosing books; Ralph and Stella had a particular librarian friend called Ronald Blythe, who was to become the famous author of *Akenfield*. He and they ran the Colchester Literary Society at which authors were invited to speak. I remember in particular Sir Ronald Storrs talking about *Lawrence of Arabia*. Colchester was less than an hour from London by LNER and writers and broadcasters enjoyed coming down for one of Stella's meals and then being paid for their talk.

Films galore!

A film club used to meet in a church hall near the library where one could see the astonishing range of Italian and French films that were being made in war-torn Europe. With English films like *The Third Man*, this was the classic period for the black-and-white ones. Ealing comedy films were always popular and, in 1947, Alexander Mackendrick, the maker of *Whisky Galore!* at Ealing Studios, had commissioned a new film script from Stella. He then invited her to bring me and Andrew to visit Ealing Studios and to watch them filming in an enormous hangar.

It was a snowy winter's day and they were shooting *The Night My Number Came Up*, which is about a British aircraft crashing on the snowy coast of Japan. The set was some four metres high and the cameras were zooming in on trolleys to record the view of the pilot through the cockpit window as the plane crashed. As a joke during a tea break, the technicians high up on the scaffolding started to throw real snowballs from the roof at their pals standing in the false snow of the set.

Stella's uncle Douglas Swanson, an engineer for the Union-Castle Line, often used to settle down on the carpet with me and Andrew to tell all about his life in the great engine room and his visits to foreign places, particularly Cape Town.

In about 1942, he had been sent with a team to Freetown in Sierra Leone, which, with its deep harbour, was a natural staging post for convoys between Britain and the Far East. An Italian liner had been raised after being scuttled in a creek. From the depths of a ship stinking of tropical sea life, Douglas and his team managed to start the engine running again and, via Rio de Janeiro, to get the hulk back to Gourock in the Clyde. His story, on which Stella aimed to base her script, was full of drama – and comedy. Sadly, Aunt Frances feared that Uncle Douglas might be prosecuted under the Official Secrets Act and, for the sake of family unity, Stella felt obliged to withdraw her proposal.

During our teens, Stella had several plays performed, most notably one on television about a bright working-class girl becoming separated from her family by going to a high school. For this, she had drawn on the experiences of Aunt Joan at an Ipswich high school full of merciless middle-class children.

Eleven +

Around Easter 1947, I was entered a year early for the first ever 'eleven-plus exam' to see if I would be selected to go to Colchester Royal Grammar School. I sat the papers with lots of other boys from other Colchester and district schools in the big hall at CRGS (where the poetry memorial reading for R. N. Currey would be held in 2002). This was a transforming moment in England's history because, for the first time, if boys and girls were selected they could go on to the grammar or high school without paying fees, and have free uniforms and free bus rides from the villages surrounding the town; it gave a selected few from all social classes the chance of a grammar and university education.

Free education was also available in secondary modern schools and technical colleges, but most of the teachers in them had been trained at teacher training colleges rather than universities. I remember that my parents looked down on them. Later in 1965 – the year Hal was born – comprehensive schools were introduced and most grammar schools were abolished. CRGS was not converted into a comprehensive school and continued to be among the top ten state schools getting pupils into Oxford and Cambridge.

The school year began on 1 September. My birthday was always a nuisance; boys and girls who took the exam in 1947 had to reach the age of 11 before 31 August; but my eleventh birthday was not until 6 September 1947, which was already into the new academic year. The 'pre' was being closed down and I would have no school to go to for a year unless I transferred to another school as Andrew, who was eight, had to do. Miss Stanyon and Ralph believed that, because I was high in the class at the 'pre', I would pass the eleven-plus; they thus arranged for me to take the exam unofficially and have it marked privately. Ralph and Stella had put my name down to board at my father's old school, Kingswood in Bath, which John Wesley had founded in 1748. I had to retake the eleven-plus exam to gain a county scholarship, which made a substantial contribution towards my fees at Kingswood and at the University of Oxford.

The same thing happened with my O Levels. The first time I took them I was legally too young to do so and then, a year later, I had to retake the three subjects I had already been studying for a year for my A Levels. Clare was born two years too early to take her O Levels and, for the two gap years, was sent to a *lycée* in Lausanne. Our daughter Tamsin was also born at the beginning of the new school year, in her case on 6 September 1967. According to Patrick Nobes, a former headmaster of Bedales, from his experience, children who are old rather than young for their year have an enormous advantage over the others. In other words, Clare, Tamsin and I might have done better had we remained in our legal age group.

The new headmaster Jack Elam agreed that in September 1947 I could go into Upper 1, the top of three first forms of about 30 boys at CRGS; there was no desk for me the first morning because I was there unofficially, but a friend from my form at the 'pre' was happy to share his with me; I felt excited and at home because half the class had come from the 'pre'. I started Greek, but it was decided that it would be better if I went to a tutor for Latin because that would be the language I would attempt, rather badly, to learn at Kingswood. A pass at School Certificate/O Level in Latin was an essential prerequisite for entry to Oxford or Cambridge. At Kingswood, a remedial class in the sixth form was organised by Adrian Bishop who engagingly made it into a club; he arranged for us to play squash.

Jack Elam, who had a close friendship with Ralph, made sure that the timetable always had free periods on Wednesday afternoons so that my father could travel up to London to record broadcasts and see publishers and editors. Jack's son Nicholas became a close friend of Andrew's and was always at 3 Beverley Road to escape having to be well-behaved in the headmaster's house. He said that it was in Ralph and Stella's house that he first saw books on sculptors like Donatello, and met writers from the Caribbean and Africa.

When later Nicholas was on the South African desk at the Foreign Office, he would read all the cables about Clare and my escape in 1964 and kept my father informed at every stage. He died aged 85 in 2024 and *The Times* carried an exceptionally interesting obituary of him. He had been given a retirement posting as British ambassador to tiny Luxembourg. He and his Dutch wife Helen, with the help of money from the Luxembourg Ministry of Culture, turned the embassy's vast basement into studios and raised funding for artists-in-residence such as Edmund de Waal, Denys Lasdun and P. D. James.

George Young, who had fought as an officer in the Green Howards regiment in the D-Day landings in Normandy, had just joined R. N. Currey's English department at CRGS. He would use a wide range of coloured chalks on the blackboard when teaching the parts of English speech; he was very good at teaching prepositions.

Our maths teacher was a tall gangling man who rejoiced in the name of Algy Batt, and who wore a dark blue suit. The word spiv, meaning dodgy, black market, or minor criminal, was much used by schoolboys when shouting at one another. I delighted the class by writing 'vips' in white chalk on his chair, which then turned into 'spiv' on the back of his blue suit.

When Ralph returned home he told us how Algy Batt had come into the staffroom during the break with 'spiv' written on his back. The other masters, who looked down on him, probably for snobbish reasons because he had not been to Oxford or Cambridge, had been laughing behind his back.

Stella's writing pays for Kingswood

I had always been told that I would be going away to board at Kingswood School in Bath, and that John Wesley, who started the evangelical Methodist movement within the Church of England, had founded it in 1748. Being the sons of Methodist ministers, for three generations most of the Martin boys had gone to Kingswood over what was to total a period of 99 years. When the train from Paddington to Bristol stopped at Bath Spa, Stella would point to the tower of Kingswood School where her husband and brothers had gone, though not her father, J. P. Martin, the author of *Uncle*.

Andrew and I could have had an outstandingly good education at Colchester Royal Grammar School, but Ralph felt it was difficult for a boy to have his father teaching at his school. He and Stella also felt that, although they had not become Methodists and had chosen to reject the Christian faith, it was of value for their sons to be able to understand Christianity and the way its stories permeate books, paintings and other works of art, history and war.

It never really occurred to me that there were fees at a public school. I had one shilling a week pocket money right up to the sixth form. I remember seeing a payslip showing that, around 1950, Ralph was being paid about £1000 as head of the English Department at CRGS. Stella had, with the help of the renowned literary agents Curtis Brown, built up as good an income as his. There would be celebration at breakfast if the post brought news of the sale of one of her stories to an American women's magazine. Sometimes, the amount was high enough to keep us at boarding school for a term. Ralph would go downstairs at 7.30 when he heard the post drop through the door; as a writer you had to expect that most of the letters would be rejection ones. Ralph and Stella would sit up in bed deciding which journal or publisher to try next. When I became a publisher I felt concerned about the effect of rejection on writers, so would try to be as encouraging as possible.

I took it for granted that women could write, although many men of my generation assumed that their work would be inferior. In 2000, Sarah Lonsdale published a book called *Rebel Women Between the Wars* in which one of those singled out is Stella Martin Currey. Her best-known book, *One Woman's Year* (1953), has recently been re-issued by Persephone, the new women's press in Bath. Stella Martin Currey drafted a biography of her father called *J. P. Martin – Father of Uncle: A Master in the Great Nonsense Tradition* (2017), which I worked on, got illustrated and published.

'But have you seen James run, sir?'

The family build-up about Kingswood was exciting before I went in September 1948. Nobody warned me that I might be homesick. I was to start in the junior house, Westwood. Years later, when headmaster of Bryanston School, the housemaster Robson

Fisher told Clare's brother Chris about how he had found a new boy, Currey, weeping into his porridge, and that even he had stopped short of getting him to finish it up. Later in the day after lunch I was dramatically sick into the gutter in Fonthill Road; I can picture the return of the diced vegetables.

I laid myself open to bullying, especially by the boys who had been at the Kingswood prep school called Prior's Court. Sedgeley, the form master of the third form, used to get boys to cut switches from the apple orchard outside for him to beat them with. One morning he was making jokes about my plumpness, but one of my classmates said, 'but have you seen him run, sir?'

Fortunately for me, I had grown early and was almost my adult height at 14. The English master Robson Fisher ran the Under Fourteens Rugby XV, which had 11 matches against other schools. When we had an away match against the City of Bath School on the other side of the valley, we would all pile onto the top deck of an ordinary bus and it took the bus conductor some time to believe that we should get the under-14 fare.

My housemaster, Gardner, made me, at 15, captain of Colts, which was the most highly regarded position in the junior school. I went on to the First Fifteen, but by then most people were catching me up in height and I was less able to stand out as a front row forward.

The 220 yards straight was the full length of the upper playing field; an eighth of a mile looks a long way from the start, but I won in the school sports. I was to become Somerset County 220 champion because the faster Kingswood runner had to take a GCSE exam that afternoon. I ran round the curve on the Bath rugby ground. I ran the 250 yards round the curve at the White City in London but started my finishing burst too early.

I caught my very first sight of Oxford when I was on my way to run on the hallowed Iffley Road track. (This was only one year after Dr Roger Bannister had run the first under four-minute mile on its cinders. When that happened a shout had resonated down the shoe locker corridor at Kingswood to the effect that 'He's done it.') The match in question had been against the Oxford

University Centipedes, which was the second team to the full blues.

On this occasion, I was to run the 220 yards low hurdles. For some strange reason, I had acquired the nickname of 'bristles' and a contemporary of mine at Kingswood amused everybody by exclaiming: 'my goodness! It is like watching an animated shaving brush.'

However, when other people grew to my height they started to beat me at athletics, which was something that I found difficult to take. I remember my brother Andrew (who was three and a half years younger than I was) coming to comfort me when I had been beaten in a race I had expected to win.

Enthused with history

In my beginning form at Kingswood – which in this case was the fourth form – the headmaster A. B. Sackett took the history class. This was because he wanted to see which boys were likely to take to the subject. He drew a plan of the Battle of Marston Moor in coloured chalks on the classroom blackboard. It involved Prince Rupert and a place called White Syke Close. I spent my last term at Kingswood studying for an essay I was preparing to enter for the Farmer prize for history. Since I was feeling doubtful about the merits of my essay, in which I tried to compare the English, French and American revolutions, so was relieved to share the prize. In the sixth form, Sackett would, like an Oxford or Cambridge tutor, get you to read your essay and then question you about it.

'Is this the outbreak of the Third World War, sir?'

In the decade after the Second World War boys were conscripted for two years' National Service. One Sunday in 1951 three of us were illicitly listening in the wireless room to news of the outbreak of the Korean War in 1950. The housemaster came in and we thought we were in trouble. A friend asked him: 'Is this the outbreak of the Third World War, sir?' and Dakin solemnly said 'Yes!' The prefect of our dormitory was one of the 1000 British troops killed in Korea, not due to fighting but because his trench caved in and the doctor was too drunk to dig him out.

TWO
To Oxford

What do I need to do to get into Oxford?

In my day, the equivalent of GCSE was called School Certificate and I was amazed that I came second in the whole of Kingswood for chemistry by learning four pages of chemical formulae. It was taught by Roche who was nicknamed 'Belsen Boche' because he told us to find the giant sequoia in the Kingswood grounds by punching the trunk of every tree until the soft red bark no longer hurt. Belsen was a Nazi concentration camp.

At A Level I took history, English and French with a view to trying for an Oxford scholarship, exhibition or undergraduate place for modern history. The English master Robson Fisher tried to talk me into taking English with him and I wish I had done as he was an inspired teacher. The headmaster, Sackett, encouraged my interest in architecture and thought I should do A-Level art, but I was worried by the standard of my drawing and of my maths, though no master could then foresee the changes computers would make for architects. I opted for A Level French, which would be useful for history at Oxford. Bishop, a friendly classics master with whom I played squash, got me into the right frame of mind to pass the hated O-Level Latin so that I could apply for Oxford or Cambridge. Sackett, the headmaster who delighted in history, used to get me to read my essays aloud to him in his study and question me as though he were an Oxford tutor. I cannot remember the name of my own history teacher who was chiefly preoccupied with courting the school nurse.

'You won't get into Oxford with those A Levels!'

My father, perhaps it was the schoolmaster in him, never gave me much praise. I remember him telling me that he and my mother thought Andrew had special talents at imaginative writing. They had high hopes of his writing skills. I accepted that they thought I was rather humdrum, at best a modest achiever.

In August 1954 my father, as a schoolmaster, was shocked by my low A-Level marks and walked me round the garden at Colchester telling me how dangerously badly I had done and doubting whether I could get into Oxford. I arrogantly said that the Oxford college entrance exams were what would matter and not A-Level marks. My father and Sackett followed up their contacts at Wadham. The three days I spent in college during the scholarship exams at Wadham staying in rooms and eating in hall were a joy, after the rugged privations of boarding school. I did want to get in.

'He interviewed us well at Wadham!'

The history tutor Pat Thompson, to whom my father had sent several boys from CRGS, wrote to my father about me and said that 'he interviewed us well.' I was used to talking to the writers and publishers who so often visited my parents. Rufus Gibson was a journalist who got me several broadcasts when the wireless was the exciting new medium through which to address the world. Henry Swanzy ran *Caribbean Voices* and *Voices from Ghana*. Jonathan Curling, director at Thomas Nelson was starting new branches in West Africa and Malaya; he had a grand manner and was known to our family as 'the Sultan'.

I was interviewed by the warden of Wadham, Sir Maurice Bowra, as Sackett had put me in for an exhibition. At that time, according to *The Times Educational Supplement*, Kingswood School got more scholarships and exhibitions than any other school, though after some years Winchester reasserted its lead. At Kingswood in those years getting the offer of a place at Wadham was regarded as a failure to get a scholarship. I was always favoured by Bowra because of my repartee. At dinner in his lodgings one night, we were discussing the novel *Les Grandes Meaunes*, and that it had been made into a film. Bowra then asked me where had I seen it and I replied, 'in Casablanca'. 'What were you doing in Casablanca?' 'I was just in Casablanca.' 'He was just in Casablanca!'

National service was a dreaded prospect. One of my father's friends in the BBC said, 'don't get stuck in the Signals at Caterick in Yorkshire. Ask to be sent to something interesting like the East African Navy or the Somaliland Camel Corps' – or 'Corpse' as it was cheerfully known. In my last year at Kingswood, I was sent over with two other contemporaries for an army medical at Bristol. After we had been examined we sat naked observing the feet of the doctors behind a glass wall who took a long time to decide our cases. A doctor came out and told me that I had been exempted from the two years of national service. I learnt later that the worry was not me going totally deaf but that I would be in a position to claim monumental damages. I was delighted that I could have a year off to travel. My father said he feared that another slump was coming, as when he went into teaching in the 1930s, and the sooner I was in a job the better. He promptly rang up Maurice Bowra and got me into Oxford that year. I was very disappointed. I had hoped to have a year off travelling.

Make sure you enjoy Oxford

I went up to Oxford in October 1955 and at Wadham found that a substantial number of undergraduates were from the grammar schools of the great Northern cities and were among the first beneficiaries of the Butler Education Act of 1944. Bowra took every chance to widen the intake. These students had state scholarships and thus an entirely free university education. I had a substantial county scholarship from Essex of about £450, which was assessed by a means test on my parents' incomes. My father advised me that I should do no more than six hours reading a day in the Bodleian or Wadham libraries from 9 to 1.00 and, after lunch games or walking from 5.00 to 7.00. After dinner, I should take advantage of clubs or meetings, but do no academic work. I should catch up on my work in the vacations at the top of our Victorian house in Colchester and not feel that I ought to earn money in vacation jobs.

I had imagined that rugby would have been more a part of my life at Oxford. I certainly was one of the outstanding freshmen players at Wadham and I enjoyed matches. I was concussed in the first match and lay on the touchline supervised by Stella and neighbour Leonie who had come to see my take-off in Oxford rugby. When we had an away match against a Cheltenham club, the two teams spent the whole evening in a pub and we only returned to Oxford late on Saturday evening. I decided to leave the team. I wanted to spend that time in Oxford with friends – men and women.

My Aunt Joan in America sent me £500 a year so that I could join clubs and take advantage of the hyperactive social life at Oxford. My father told me that when he was at Wadham as the son of a Wesleyan minister, he was poor and had taken the Methodist pledge against alcohol. He was certain that Aunt Joan's money would help me feel freer about social events. The established social practice in 1956 was that men invited women out and paid for the meal in a restaurant. There were about seven men to every woman undergraduate, so there was much competition.

Oxford reconciliation with Germany

Ian Wright had come up to Oxford two years earlier to Christ Church from Kingswood where he had a reputation as an elegant fixer of schemes and conspiracies. On the first Sunday he took me to a meeting of the Oxford International Committee, which was held in style over lunch in a private room at the Taj Mahal in the Turl, the first Indian restaurant in Oxford.

Ten years after the end of the Second World War a group of dons were working to build reconciliation with German universities and they got the British Council to pay for a two-week conference each Easter vacation in an Oxford college. Once it was Balliol, another time Somerville, but the best was leafy Lincoln in the Turl. To justify this elegant holiday camp for both women and men, Prue Hiller (later Prue Nichols) and I got together a programme of thirty lectures on 'Britain: Past Present and Future'. We had an Oxford dark blue letterhead, with the vice-chancellor and rows of Oxford worthies printed across the top. It was so impressive that we only had one rejection letter to our invitations in three years. We paid expenses, but no fees, to academics and well-known people from the arts, politics and journalism.

My parents Ralph and Stella Currey delighted in passing on suggestions from their London journalist and literary friends. Sir Maurice Bowra, the warden of Wadham said, 'Yes, dear boy' as he walked across the quad and every year made the subject of Oxford University entertaining, at least to English undergraduates. The most extraordinary contributor was the artist Stanley Spencer, who was driven over from his cow-filled Cookham residence by the mother of one of the committee members.

Nigel Nicolson and I sat in an entirely empty meeting room at Somerville and he said it wasn't the first time that he had had no audience. Then, 20 minutes late, suddenly the room filled with delegates. The committee had taken them to an English magistrate's court in session in the Town Hall and they were not allowed to leave until a case had finished. Brutalist architects Alison and Peter Smithson (Economist Building) arrived in a VW Beetle – at that time considered an exotic car in England – with three-year-old Simon (later to design Madrid airport) bouncing up and down in the luggage slot behind the back seat.

'Another nice man to take me punting!'

In the 1950s there was a boom in English language schools that attracted glamorous students from across postwar Europe and Latin America. The British Council was anxious for them to meet students from the colleges. Undergraduates were inclined to be exclusive and look down on foreigners.

On 11 May 1956, in the first summer term, they put on a party at Black Hall, the manor house at the top of St Giles. George Cacanas from Worcester introduced me to Clare Wilson and Gilia Slocock from St Anne's, whom he knew from the Worcester Reels Club. I immediately formed a bond with Clare Wilson because she and I had both failed the preliminary exam in modern history, which meant that if one failed the retake one would be out of the university. She had failed the French and Latin although she had spent two years at a *lycée* in Lausanne.

As George and I crossed St Giles after leaving the party, I asked about Clare with interest. Her memory of me was of 'another nice man to take me punting!' Punting indeed provided a cheerful form of encounter when women's and men's colleges were still segregated. During the summer term, Joan's money did indeed give me the freedom to take her out to dinner. We took long walks on Port Meadow. I was named by Clare's friends as 'Faithful James'.

Gabrielle McCracken wrote in *St Anne's Journal* that Clare 'was a tall good-looking girl with dark hair in a bun and her own distinctive style of dress; not for her the rigid fashion of the 1950s, of tight waist, full skirt, permed hair.' She kept a visitor's book in her room and I was given a season ticket because I came so often. She had her twenty-first birthday party at Studleigh Priory and put herself at the head of the table with her two favoured admirers on either side. Both of us were deaf in opposing ears so she had to take care about the seating.

Sir Maurice Bowra asked me before I retook Prelims whether I had failed French or Latin and when I said I had failed both the modern history papers, his response was 'Grotesque! Grotesque!' My tutor Lawrence Stone was formidable.

I would spend each of the eight weeks of term in the Bodleian Library Radcliffe Camera reading and making tight notes on the books and academic articles on his reading list. After dinner on Sunday, I would take until midnight to write my essay. On Monday morning, I would stagger up the circular staircase that led to Stone's room above the Wadham gateway. In the seventeenth century, it had been Christopher Wren's observatory where he had had his telescope in the room when he was Savilian Professor of Astronomy. I would proceed to read my essay to Stone. He would sink further and further into his armchair.

Then there would be a string of fearsome exclamations against my essay. 'Shit! Shit! Absolute shit!' With heart pounding and adrenalin rushing, I would try to defend my work. I had produced rushed essays for Stone and failed to provide references to show that I had consulted all the books on his reading list.

There are no university exams during the second year and I had taken advantage of that to become a feature's editor of *Isis* and president of the Oxford International Committee with its conferences for foreign students. And to spend as much time as possible with Clare.

'All children of psychiatrists are mad!'

Just outside Colchester there was a substantial mental hospital called Severalls. Our group of young people included quite a few whose parents worked there.

Early on with Clare I made one of those dangerous sweeping statements, namely that 'all children of psychiatrists are mad.' And she said, 'what do you think I am?' I told her she was the daughter of a doctor. It turned out that Henry Wilson had a psychiatrist's practice in Harley Street with members of the establishment among his patients. In 1916 during the First World War he had registered as a conscientious objector. He had to appear before a tribunal of conservative magistrates and was sent to pick potatoes in Lincolnshire. A hundred years ago Freudian psychiatry was new and treated with suspicion. So he was very much a pioneer.

'You are intellectually incapable of getting a second!'

For the final year in modern history one chose a special subject and was given a list of original documents in the Bodleian to study; it was the most exciting part of the course. I opted for Cromwell and the civil war, which unfortunately was taught at Wadham by Lawrence Stone. The Oxford final examinations had four classes. If undergraduates were struggling they were given the chance to cut the special subject and resign themselves to a third- or fourth-class degree. Archie Crawford's family were renowned biscuit makers in Carlisle and had given substantial money to Wadham, so he had been allowed in for a third or fourth.

Lawrence Stone walked me one summer morning round the marvellous Fellows Garden and said, 'you are intellectually incapable of getting a second!' I modestly accepted his judgement and agreed I should drop the special subject. However, at the beginning of the vacation, when I told my schoolmaster father Ralph and schoolmaster Uncle Hal, they told me to get on the train to Oxford and go and see the more liberal history tutor Pat Thompson, and tell him I was going to work for a second. My father said if I went into teaching, the Burnham scale would pay more for a second.

In February 1958 I was working in my third-floor of digs in Museum Road when I saw Clare cycle up on her granny bike and post in a letter. I knew she was telling me that we should not go on seeing one another. I had expected the message and it made me concentrate on making sure I got a second. My tutor Pat

Thompson told me that I had done best in European history. In the exam, when you looked through the paper you chose three questions and then as a fourth something on which you could start to write with great interest. There was a question about why Amsterdam had taken over from Antwerp. For my fourteenth birthday Edith Currey had given me a book called *The Sea Around Us* by Rachel Carson, which showed how global warming had attracted herrings into the Baltic. She presented a great rhythm in sevens. In the fourteenth century there were wolves in Paris and in the next century the world will begin to cool for 700 years. I seemed to have interested the examiner and got 'a good second'.

Discovering France and Italy

In 1951 the Currey family had been invited by the Spaak family to visit Morocco – hardly known at that time in England. At the age of 14 I was deeply impressed by Marielle who was a year older than me and much more sophisticated. She did make me concentrate on learning to speak French, though with limited success. Her letters to me were in fluent English. I did rather well in my written French A Level and came to read Maupassant stories with considerable ease. French was needed for my modern history documents in the Bodleian.

Wadham arranged for me to have a French tutor, a dramatically elegant Franciscan called Dominic de Grunne, who at Easter in the second year selected me to go for six weeks to a French liqueur manufacturer's family house and talk to him in English because he was faced with making a speech in English at the Rotary International in Geneva in August. His sweet liqueur was called La Verveine du Velay and it was made in the mountain town of Le Puy-en-Velay in the Auvergne.

Dominic de Grunne had arranged for me to work for six weeks in the tourist office through which some local lace manufacturers paid me to take British and American tourists to buy the town's speciality. All in all, I had two months of mostly speaking

French. I was supposed to speak English to the French teenage children, but it suited me that they were not keen. I was even provided with the family Vespa scooter, which I fell off and ran skid marks up my face. A tombstones engraver laughed and asked me if I had '*dérappé sur le gravillon?*'

I then went hitch-hiking in Italy for a month looking for the outstanding Italian modern buildings being featured in the *Architectural Review*. On the way back to Paris, I was head of a line of hitch-hikers in the early morning outside Cannes. After a few minutes, an elegant French woman stopped and addressed the first three of us in the queue. She explained that she always went along the line to select a French speaker so she would have somebody to talk to. We got on well and she dropped me off at the youth hostel in Mâcon for the night and picked me up the next morning. She actually lived in Chartres and dropped me there for a first visit. When I picked up my wages in Le Puy-en-Velay, they almost covered the entire cost of my Italian trip. Breakfast was coffee and a doughnut; nothing at midday; and the pasta in the evening could be very cheap. I was so thin and hungry by the time I reached Colchester that my parents said that at the first meal I demolished a whole loaf of bread.

Siena

In August 1965, when I was in the student house (*casa dello studente*) in Florence, a group of Americans persuaded me to go with them to the horse race in Siena known as *Il Palio*. It is run round the Piazza del Campo, a great triangular space in front of the Town Hall. Every district (*contrada*) in Siena enters horses and bareback riders. Our group got ourselves into the area by the finish line where the crowd swung as a mass. It was like Shakespeare's *Julius Caesar*, in which 'the crowd threw up their sweaty nightcaps and uttered such a mass of stinking breath'.

Clare and I loved Siena more than any other Italian city and stayed there several times in a hotel looking over the city wall across the Tuscan countryside. In 2025 there was an exhibition in the National Gallery in London of Sienese paintings from around 1400. The background of these painting shows a town that has the same style today.

Isis *and Suez and Bosch*

Isis was the most prestigious Oxford university magazine. It was founded in 1892 with offices above the printer who owned it; and it made a lot of money out of advertising for the prosperous undergraduate market. I volunteered for the *Isis* news reporting team under Joan Thomas who sent me to report on a talk to be given by the poet Stephen Spender.

The dominance of Stephen Spender in the world of poetry publishing annoyed my father, the well-established poet R. N. Currey. Poets in England looked down on those from the colonies, such as Roy Campbell, from whom Spender lived in fear of outrageous homophobic attacks in print and at meetings.

At Oxford in 1957, with characteristic Etonian entitlement, Stephen Hugh-Jones assumed the editorship of *Isis*, one of the most desired undergraduate positions. I did not know him, but one day in the second term, before he took over as editor, to my surprise he appeared at my rooms in Wadham. He said he had been impressed by my Stephen Spender piece, and wanted me to become an *Isis* features editor and to run a literary news page each week under the name of 'Bosch'. He hated the previous *Isis* social-gossip column, which was full of photos of undergraduates who in their black ties had sprung from the fashionable Edmark photographers in the High Street.

For each of the eight weeks of the term, he wanted me to write and edit a whole-page spread across three columns of type. He assumed that my account of Spender showed an unpleasant savagery and that I would give sharp reports on events surrounding newly emerging literary writings in the colleges and university at large. My friends throughout the university fed me ample stories, but then attacked me if I used them in *Isis*. I thought that one of my best lines was, 'meanwhile, down at the Worcester Country Club'. Needless to say, this infuriated my Worcester friends. As the term went on, I found the task more and more demanding each week and Stephen Hugh-Jones had to fill gaps. The editorship certainly taught me that I was not hard enough to be a journalist.

Because my deaf ear exempted me from national service, I was at least two years younger than the other features editors on *Isis*. Two years difference in confidence at that age is enormous, and I was in awe of them for their informed world views. *Isis* often featured in the national newspapers. When the British went into Suez on 29 October 1956, editors William Miller and Paul Thompson felt they ought to publish in *Isis* what they had learnt on the army Russian course during their national service about the Soviet Empire; they were sentenced to three months in prison for breaking the 1911 Official Secrets Act. The Wadham senior common room was practically alone in thinking that the British invasion was a mistake.

Getting a job

In the summer term of the third year I visited Miss Fone's office for career advice and expressed an interest in journalism, broadcasting and publishing, and she in turn sent details about possible jobs to me at Wadham. There were so many applications for a traineeship in the BBC that it was even considered an achievement to have been chosen to go for an interview with a gentleman noted for having been a rowing blue. Melvyn Bragg from Wadham was chosen the next year and he has become renowned for the BBC Radio 4 programme *In Our Time*. The general publisher André Deutsch sounded attractive, but my father pointed to a remark on the bottom line of the information sheet saying that there was no pay. The job was for what nowadays we call 'an intern'.

Offered two jobs

Having usurped the pre-war Bauhaus tradition in the 1950s, Italy now led the world in modern design. During my second long vacation, I hitch-hiked around Italy to look for these exciting new buildings. Noting that the great glass windows of Rome railway station followed the sweep of the Roman wall outside it, I wrote two substantial articles for *Isis* on Italian design and, for the photograph, had to persuade our printer owners reluctantly to buy full-page half-tone printer plates from *The Architectural Review*. Hulton Press was the leading Fleet Street publisher of magazines when *Picture Post* was the top selling illustrated journal in the days before television took hold. On the strength of my *Isis* articles on Italian design, I was offered a paid vacation job for a fortnight at the journals *Studio* and *Art and Industry*. When I was offered a job at Oxford University Press, Hulton Press promptly offered me one on its *Art and Industry* magazine, but I wanted the chance to travel and was inclined to publishing rather than journalism.

THREE
Oxford University Press & South Africa

Oxford University Press asks, 'where would you like to go?'

I had a most enjoyable interview with David Bickmore at the cartographic department of Oxford University Press at the top of St Giles. He was delighted when I told him how in 1951, for my fifteenth birthday, I had asked to be given the new *Oxford Atlas* with its attractive style of map-making developed during the war by Cook, Hammond and Kell Ltd. At the end of an hour he said he really was looking for a geography graduate, but as I was interested more generally in publishing he would pass my name on to his colleagues.

I was summoned to a second interview and turned up in St Giles only to be told that it was to be with the secretary in Walton Street. As a male, I immediately assumed the secretary would be female and junior. I was lent an umbrella, as it was pouring with rain, and rushed round to Oxford University Press. I was led, late and wet, into a grand office with a charming donnish man behind an enormous desk. What I did not know was that Colin Roberts, the secretary to the delegates of Clarendon Press, was head of OUP worldwide. After a pleasant interview he said he would give my name to OUP headquarters in Amen House.

There, in the shadow of St Paul's and the Stationers' Hall, I had an interview with the publisher John Brown in his magnificent eighteenth-century office. Parnwell, the deputy publisher, asked me, 'where would you like to go?' This was an exciting prospect to be offered at the age of 23. I replied 'India, South Africa or America – anywhere but Australia or New Zealand!' 'Nobody has asked to go to South Africa before!' he exclaimed. 'Why do you want to go there?' ' 'I have a South African grandmother and I am interested to find out about apartheid.'

At interviews there is usually a hidden agenda. They needed an editor in Cape Town because it was planned that the editor David Philip was to open an office in Salisbury, Southern Rhodesia. It helped that my father knew several people in OUP. In fact, OUP had published his first book of verse, *Tiresias and Other Poems* in 1940, with an elegant cover designed by his school contemporary Lynton Lamb, who was on the way to being one of the most admired typographers and chosen to design the leather binding for the Queen's coronation Bible. While in the Indian Army, my father had worked on an anthology of soldiers' poetry with Philip Chester, who had become the deputy publisher in charge of OUP branches in the dominions, as the white Commonwealth was then called.

I had got on well with the personnel manager, Jimmy Hughes-Davis, and slipped in to ask him about what to expect in the fifth interview, which was scheduled to be with the secretary of Clarendon Press in Oxford. He said all three candidates would be offered traineeships to go to branches across the world and that the publisher wanted to show the secretary what a fine trio they had chosen in Hugo Brunner, Stewart Melluish and myself.

Hugo Brunner said he thought that we were three rivals for one job and viewed us both with hostility as we waited for the interview. We all three shared an office at the back of Amen House, which had a window looking down on the yard at the side of the Old Bailey courts. The lower part of the glass was frosted. If there was a renowned trial we would stand on our desks to see the accused being led in handcuffs from the Black Maria. At lunchtime, instead of going to a pub, the three of us would set off to visit selected Wren churches in the City.

Hugo Brunner, a delightful old Etonian, expected to operate at a higher level than I did. He was from the Brunner family, as in Brunner Mond & Company, the chemical manufacturers that later became Imperial Chemical Industries (ICI). He said on our first day that 'the trouble with Oxford University Press is that it does not have directors.' I did not even know what a 'director' was. Hugo's mother commissioned a son et lumière performance at her castle manor house in Oxfordshire with an inscription by the poet Robert Gittings saying 'This Tower My Prison'. Hugo took me there one evening to be on the gate collecting entrance fees. Hugo was sent to run Oxford University Press in Hong Kong, where he went walking with Clare's brother Lyn who called his second son Hugo after him. He later was able to buy and save the renowned literary publisher Chatto & Windus. I never expected to know somebody who was to become Lord Lieutenant of Oxfordshire.

OUP *an agreeable college of publishing*

My parents had always been hospitable to our English-speaking South African relations. Two came to stay with us after being released from a prisoner-of-war camp in Germany. My parents took a cousin from Natal to Constable country at Dedham with walks along the River Stour. We got ourselves lost in the green lanes, so he went off to find the bus back; we were delighted when he suddenly appeared hanging out of a double-decker bus as though he had captured it.

My South African relations were marvellously friendly and seriously reactionary, and it panicked me to think of having to work with white English-speaking people like them. Fortunately, during the autumn of 1958, I had read *South African Winter* in which the author, James Morris, portrayed what an extraordinarily varied place the country was – brown, white and black. In a whole chapter devoted to liberal Afrikaners in Stellenbosch, he described having dinner with the very person with whom I was going to work, the historian Leo Marquard and his wife Nell.

Oxford University Press in London was an agreeable college

of publishing, with young men arriving and going to places across the world. There were many young women working as editors and secretaries, but they were not yet being sent to the overseas offices. I was able to rent a room in a house in Chelsea on condition I went home for the weekend to my parents in Colchester. On Monday mornings I would have scrambled eggs on toast in the dining car on my way back to Liverpool Street. I paid for myself to go to evening classes in typography at the Central School of Arts and Crafts where the tutor showed us how he had laid out Ernst Gombrich's highly illustrated *The Story of Art*.

Oxford University Press had realised that the end of empire would bring a need for new syllabuses and new textbooks. It recruited three trainees a year such as myself to publish new textbooks and train new staff. Ghana had gained independence in 1957. Just after I arrived in South Africa in October 1959, the Conservatives under Macmillan won the British election. There was much rejoicing in white South Africa, but Conservative policy was no different from Labour's. In fact, when Macleod was appointed Secretary of State for the Colonies, he immediately speeded up decolonisation in six African colonies. Britain could not afford the costs of another Kenyan Mau Mau revolt or Malayan emergency. However, apartheid in South Africa was going to last until 1989.

'You are really concerned about those books, aren't you?'

During our nine-month training, we would be sent for six weeks to the Oxford University Press warehouse at Neasden. This was fascinating as it made one realise how books actually reached readers across the world. It is easy to publish books. It is difficult to sell them. There was an enormous glass atrium for the 'the Computer' with staff in white overalls as acolytes. When Clare and I bought our first personal computer in the 1980s it would have been more powerful than that of OUP's main frame.

I was put in the hands of a hospitable looker-out. When orders came in all books in stock were looked out from its shelf, invoiced and packed. Any books not in stock were recorded as 'dues' to wait for the title to come back into stock. I realised that the dues, even when they came back in stock, were not being supplied to the annoyed waiting customers. To keep myself occupied I focused on the piles of books dues that had been left unsupplied. The trouble was that the bonus scheme concentrated on new orders. My looker-out one day near the end of six weeks looked at me and said, in tones of amazement – 'you really care about those books, don't you?' I gave my ideas to the management about how dues could be interlocked into the bonus scheme.

To the Cape

One weekend my mother and I were washing up when my father came in and found us both weeping. My mother said, 'James has been told when he must leave for South Africa.' It was complicated because a well-established manager was aiming, after a three-week run in Birmingham, to give Stella's play, *French Polish*, a full West End run whenever a theatre became available.

OUP generously allowed me to delay my departure and fly. I thus avoided travelling for 13 days on a Union Castle liner playing deck quoits with people like my reactionary relations. Oxford University Press flew me to South Africa in 24 hours in a turboprop Brittania that came down at Rome, Tripoli, Khartoum, Nairobi, Salisbury and Johannesburg and then on to Cape Town. The fare came to more than my annual salary.

Randolph Vigne and Patrick Duncan

Randolph Vigne and Patrick Duncan were to be the two most important people for me in South Africa. Tim Holmes and I, young and single, responded to their ever-inventive politics. We were always available for any clandestine work.

In July 1959 I set about finding somewhere to live. Cape Town offered about three possible choices, but I opted for the historic centre of the city where the early settlements of Jan van Riebeeck and the Dutch East India Company had first become established in the bowl under Table Mountain. Randolph Vigne put me in touch with his friends Joy and Anthony Millar who lived in a handsome house with a vast stoep – the South African word for a veranda – that had been built in 1840 overlooking the historic city and Table Bay. The Millars had converted the servants' quarters into a compact and stylish flat behind the coolness and privacy of shutters at the back, which suited me perfectly.

Gillian and Randolph Vigne lived in Clifton, where the houses are built on the steep mountain slopes running down to the cold Atlantic Ocean. There is a commuter railway running eastwards towards the Southern Suburbs where the houses face the warmer Indian Ocean. Patrick and Cynthia Duncan lived on that side and had a swimming pool the shape of Africa.

Baasskaap and violence

Of course I had arrived in South Africa aware of apartheid, but to witness it in action was a shock. An Afrikaans woman with English as thick as her forearm, who runs the dry cleaners, tells a black man to wait to be dealt with because she has 'not got time to find his things'. She finds time to locate the belongings of two white people. She dosed me with molasses, but raised her voice if she addressed a black person. In the butchers somebody said, 'I would shoot the kaffirs and they would come back to work the next day!' I was in the squash club when the Shell executive, who was getting changed next to me, said, 'I believe in the lynch principle!' It is a society run on the constant threat of violence. I read that in 1957 there were more murders a day in South Africa than for the whole year in New Zealand. The daily average in South

OXFORD UNIVERSITY PRESS & SOUTH AFRICA

Apartheid here! Apartheid there! A typical sign.

Africa is five, whereas there are only four for the whole year in New Zealand.

History of the resistance to apartheid

It was only 11 years before I arrived in South Africa in 1959 that the National Party had won the whites-only election in 1948 with its policy of legal racial segregation called apartheid (or apartness). The opposition United Party supported a colour bar that protected white access to certain jobs. The Suppression of Communism Act was passed in 1950. From 1952 Africans were issued with what was nicknamed the *dom* (stupid) pass and a campaign of passive resistance against carrying passes started in 1952. The Liberal Party was founded in 1953 by, among others, Alan Paton. He was the author of the novel *Cry, the Beloved Country*, which had brought South Africa to international attention at the time of the National Party victory in 1948. The African National

Congress (ANC) was established in 1911 and now was led by Chief Albert Luthuli. In 1959, the Pan-African Congress led by Robert Sobukwe had just split from the ANC because it felt it had been captured by white communists. Also in 1959, the Progressive Party broke away from the United Party, so there were changes in black and white politics.

In March 1960 at Sharpeville the police reacted to a non-violent anti-pass campaign by shooting into the backs of 69 Pan-African Congress campaigners. The government had demonstrated that it would always resort to violence. Recent research by Stephen Ellis has found that, in reaction to the Sharpeville massacre, at least 23 underground organisations decided that the policy of non-violence had failed. Mandela formed Umkonto we Sizwe as the armed wing of the ANC. In *South Africa Belongs to Us*, Francis Meli describes the history of the ANC and its dialectic with the Communist Party. In 1961, Randolph Vigne and others clandestinely set up the African Resistance Movement (ARM) to plan for sabotage to be used when politically necessary. It was to be more than thirty years before change became possible in South Africa, after the fall of the Berlin Wall in 1989 and the collapse of Russian imperialism. A period of transition followed and in 1994 there were fully free elections on a universal franchise.

Brecht's Caucasian Chalk Circle

Cape Town did not then have a professional theatre company, so when I saw an announcement in the newspaper that the director of Belgium's Flemish National Theatre was holding auditions for a local production, I decided to apply. To my surprise, I got selected as a soldier. It would be a good way of getting to meet some young South Africans and to help manage my homesickness. Rehearsals were for six weeks and there were performances every night for three weeks and twice on Saturday. I was a very English soldier being ordered around by an Afrikaner corporal. The director made us the comic turn of the evening. *Die Burger* described the humour as 'unintended', but our producer had worked out how to get every laugh out of the clash between Afrikaans and English accents. The *Cape Times* described it as 'a rare theatrical treat' and it had the longest run ever at the theatre and highest percentage of seats sold. My parents had subscribed to the airmail edition of the London *Times*, which I was glad to have to read in the long waits in the dressing room.

R. N. Currey wins the South African poetry prize

R. N. Currey, Sidney Clouts and Anthony Delius shared the first South African poetry prize in 1960. In September, I took my parents on a lecture tour of the English departments of South African universities. My manager Leo Marquard helpfully made contact with his network, and my father gave several lectures in Cape Town. In Pietermaritzburg in Natal, he gave a Settler's Day lecture in the open-air stadium, which widely reported. He wrote, 'we have gone unarmed among a strange variety of Phipsons, some more like Wild West characters than I have ever seen.' Stella was also asked to give various lectures and broadcasts.

On the road from Pietermaritzburg to Underberg we visited a farm where my grandmother Edith Vinnicombe spent her childhood with Mary Phipson. This was while, as my father described it in his *Vinnicombe's Trek*, her parents moved from dorp to dorp building Dutch Reformed churches. At the farm they still had one of the great wagons used not only on the farm but also for transport riding from the coast and into the Transvaal and on to Rhodesia. They were towed by six oxen or six horses. Clare and I found a wagon there in 2012; elegant and slim and made from silver-grey seasoned oak. Although the Afrikaners have usurped the image of the trek wagon, everybody had to depend on wagons, much as we depend on trucks and lorries today.

The silver seasoned oak of the great wagon that rolled from Durban to Pietermaritzburg and up to Rhodesia.

It had a touch of the monumental

The visit in 1960 to my grandfather John Currey's circuit in Ermelo in the Transvaal was my only substantial experience during my time in South Africa of an Afrikaner dorp. It had been forgotten how much apartheid there was between the white tribes. Stella was shown photograph upon photograph of mayors in the mayor's parlour. My father Ralph, the son of a Wesleyan Methodist minister, had been good friends with the son of the Dutch Reformed Church's dominee, who was now a dominee himself, living in what Stella described as a bishop's palace. My father thought I ought to have learnt Afrikaans, but I told him that I would rather have learnt Xhosa.

The BBC Home Service commissioned R. N. Currey to present a programme called *Early Morning in Vaaldorp*. *The Sunday Times* in London gave it a wonderful review:

> In short, 'the laager mentality' emerged without the author making the point; his form was semi-dramatic, but the characters never seemed to be propping up the narrative. Mr

Ronald Blythe (left) and R. N. Currey (right) at the launch of Vinnicombe's Trek.

Currey is no propagandist. He almost chanted his words, fully aware that he was speaking something out of the ordinary but never giving you the impression that he was out of the ordinary. ... His script reminded me of Patrick White's great Australian novel *Voss*. It had a touch of the monumental.

Macmillan's 'Wind of Change' speech

On 3 February 1960, British Prime Minister Harold Macmillan gave a speech to the South African House of Assembly in which he told the National Party that 'the wind of change is blowing through this continent' and that South Africa would have to get rid of apartheid if it were going to stay in the Commonwealth. Macmillan made it clear to Verwoerd that, if South Africa declared itself a republic, all the Commonwealth countries would have to agree whether to invite it back and not just Britain. According to Anthony Delius, who was in the press gallery at the time, Verwoerd became increasingly pale and stumbled into his answer.

Joy Millar, in whose house I had a flat, behaved at the gates of Parliament in a way calculated to incense all Afrikaners. In her dramatically flowing dress she rushed through the police cordon and right up to Macmillan's open-air Rolls Royce and called out right across Verwoerd: 'what a *won*derful speech!' She was a splendidly impulsive woman.

President of the League of Nations

Stella's literary agent Kitty Black was a South African and she gave me introductions to several distinguished South Africans. One of the people who invited me out was Charles de Water who had been the South African high-commissioner in London in the 1930s. He had designed South Africa House in Trafalgar Square, which stands at right angles to the National Gallery. He had to attend in Paris, the forerunner of the United Nations, the League of Nations, of which for a time he became president. He was pleased to show me round his collection of South African artists like Pierneef, whom he had patronised when in London. He also showed me his collection of South African wines, but said he could not drink them because of his gout. I said that was a pity. He replied: 'It's more than a pity. It's a tragedy!'

Book design and David Philip

I wanted to get a job in publishing but I was mostly interested in book design and typography. I had taken all chances at *Isis* to work on paste ups. I had enquired about going to the London College of Printing, and went to evening classes at the Central School of Arts and Crafts in London. However, as I was an arts graduate, I was expected to do editorial work. In Cape Town David Philip was also interested in typography but he was being sent to Salisbury to open an office in what was then Rhodesia. Leo Marquard in Cape Town left all the editing and design to me, so I could organise my own apprenticeship. I learnt a lot from the two printers we mostly used. It was so valuable to be able to talk to the, mostly Monotype, typesetters themselves. I also designed or commissioned some thirty covers and jackets a year, but the greatest job of all was laying out the 24-page monthly review for the *New African*, its name in homage to the *New Statesman*.

A bicycle powered press, the Nazis and John Donne

The outstanding English language publisher at the Cape was a Dutchman called A. A. Balkema. He had a large shop below ground in a house near the Dutch East India Company's Garden. I used to take my typographical layouts to show him while he ate his lunchtime sandwiches. The Balkemas had managed to survive in the Netherlands during the war doing humdrum jobs such as printing forms for the Nazi administration. Mrs Balkema was large and had an exercise bike in the front room, which generated electricity for the clandestine press in the basement where, for pure enjoyment, Balkema kept setting and printing such works as John Donne's poetry in an elegant English secret edition.

District Six and Dollar Brand

Every Sunday evening there was a great gathering of young people of all colours for Dollar Brand's band. He was later to become internationally known as Abdullah Ibrahim. District Six is near the docks and, under the Group Areas Act, was classed as Coloured. It is the heart of working-class Cape Town. A friend Sally Morgan risked imprisonment for the affair she conducted with the Cape photographer Joseph Louw who had a flat on Hanover Street. It helped that she was Jewish and quite dark, but they both risked jail.

Randolph Vigne and delight in Transkei history

Randolph and I spent a July 1961 morning walking round Lion's Head and the wild places behind his house. He showed an antiquarian's delight in Pondoland history, which enabled him to get on with the chiefs when he disappeared into the Transkei to work for the Liberals. On such occasions, when Gillian was expecting their second child, I used to overnight at Clifton House in case she went into labour early. From the bath, Gillian would shout, 'I am bloody well not going to have this baby until Randolph gets back from the Transkei.' Inevitably, though, Lucy had different ideas and her labour did indeed start early. Fortunately, Dr

Kok lived just down the steps below Clifton House, which was auspicious because he was later able to save Gillian's life during a severe asthma attack.

Patrick Duncan and Contact

Patrick Duncan, renowned son of a former governor-general, founded, owned and edited *Contact*, a political newspaper that every other week cheered us with its reports and photographs of decolonisation in African countries to the north as they became independent. The *Contact* office at the top of Parliament Chambers opposite the Houses of Parliament in Cape Town was the gathering point for every Liberal. There were meetings, talks and parties.

Cynthia Duncan had been born an Ashley Cooper, the family that founded the Bank of England. Her wealth enabled Patrick Duncan to start *Contact*. He also had both financial and professional journalistic support from David Astor, editor and owner of the *Observer*, the most radical and stylish London newspaper of the day.

Patrick Duncan immediately involved me in *Contact* and put me on its editorial board. My main contribution was drawing political maps as needed when events unfolded in Africa to the north as countries became independent and as conflicts broke out. My typography was influenced by the *Observer*.

My maps depended on the new Swedish invention of Letraset rub-down lettering and its sudden drop in price from £3 a sheet to about 60 pence. The *Contact* freedom calendar as a centrefold of the magazine became a feature. Each year I blacked in the countries as they became independent so that the flood of black advanced down Africa towards the white redoubt of the British Federation of Rhodesia and Nyasaland and of South Africa itself. The enclaves of Basutoland (Lesotho), Bechuanaland (Botswana) and Swaziland were still British, which meant they provided legal refuge for people fleeing from South Africa. Patrick Duncan was thrilled with it. When Stanley Uys, the correspondent for *The Sunday Times* (Johannesburg) and *Observer*, brought the local correspondent for Deutsche Welle into *Contact*, they quickly snaffled copies.

David and Marie Philip

On my first day, David Philip, who was a descendant of the famous missionary Dr John Philip, took me out to lunch at Garlicks, one of Cape Town's more prestigious department stores. On telling me that, 'when I joined the press I felt "I don't want to leave the press until the day I die",' I was a little embarrassed by the extent of his enthusiasm. I just felt pleased to have got a first job in a renowned company for three years in a fascinating part of the world. I certainly knew I wanted to go back to England and hoped for a job in the London office or to find another job in London publishing.

The OUP office in Cape Town was on the north-facing side of a plain ten-storey office block built on the reclaimed land called the Foreshore near Duncan Docks, named after Patrick Duncan's father. There were two departments, trade and editorial. Freddie Cannon – cheerful, British and reactionary – was the trade manager selling academic books not only for OUP but also for some of the best American university presses. He had also built up contacts with some of the British general bookshop publishers like Jonathan Cape, John Murray and Hamish Hamilton. He was very well regarded in the bookshops across South Africa and, as a conservative, was afraid that they would be offended by Leo Marquard's academic titles attacking apartheid.

Leo Marquard had built up a distinguished academic list, which OUP distributed across the world. In the 1920s he had founded NUSAS, the campaigning students union, and then in 1953 the South African Liberal Party with Alan Paton. He felt I had been imposed on him and was quite reserved towards me for the first six months of my time in the country. That, however, changed during the crisis following the Sharpeville massacre when everybody started to exchange news and rumours on a daily basis. When in September 1960 my father came on a lecture tour of South African universities, Marquard told him that he was very pleased with me – though not to tell me that.

FOUR
Just in Time for the Revolution

A revolution in South Africa would never happen in the summer. In the Cape everybody would be on the beaches. The Sharpeville massacre was at the beginning of autumn. There were times in that first year when I was to think that I had arrived just in time for the revolution. The South African police were trained for confrontation rather than collaboration. In the Cape in late March there was a ten-day build up of tension between the police and the striking Africans in the Langa township. By 5.45 on 21 March 1960 a crowd of 50,000 had built up within Langa. The police tried to disperse them by driving their Saracen armoured cars directly into the crowds, and they shot and killed four people.

Randolph Vigne and the New African

I had first had a long talk with Randolph Vigne in October 1959 on the dramatic stoep of Joy and Anthony Millar's house. We were amused to find that we had both been at Wadham and had both admired the warden Sir Maurice Bowra, who would send us Christmas cards in South Africa containing notes such as 'keep your escape routes clear!'

As the literary editor of *Contact*, Randolph Vigne had more material than he could publish, so decided to start a new monthly journal. The *New Statesman* was the leading radical journal in London, and it was this that led me to suggest calling it the *New African*; then one Saturday I designed its headband featuring clothes hanger men. Neville Rubin secured money in London, Geneva and Paris to keep it funded. Editorial work was done by Tim Holmes, who had been at Trinity College, Oxford and was an editor of *Contact*. (Once he said to me as I entered his office: 'you have just missed Him.' 'Him' was Nelson Mandela.)

A cluster of friends round Contact

The *Contact* office was in the Parliament Buildings opposite the Houses of Parliament. Val Bijl was secretary of the Liberal Party, which had an office in the same building. Tim Holmes was the editor of *Contact*. He had been at Trinity College, Oxford at the same time as I had been at Wadham.

Over the long university vacation of 1959–60, Patrick Duncan had given Mary Kirwood, from the university in Pietermaritzburg, a temporary job on *Contact*. She captured all the men. Val said 'Mary, Mary, quite contrary, with little men all in a row.'

The communist lawyer Albie Sachs was a close friend; he was to draft the constitution for the new South Africa. Joseph Louw, the photographer from Cape Town's District Six, was to capture the assassination of Martin Luther King in Memphis with its forest of arms pointing at the gunman.

Mary had a friend who grew Christmas trees up on the edge of the forest below Table Mountain. We called in and he pressed us to take one. As we went back to the car we provoked a whole chorus of cheers and shouts from the standby gangs at the sight of a Christmas tree walking down the valley.

In convoy with Mary to Natal

In early 1960 I was due to set off for an Oxford University Press visit to schools and universities in Grahamstown and the Eastern Cape and the Transkei bantustan capital at Umtata. I was to use the OUP's enormous American Dodge. After her Christmas at the Cape, Mary Kirwood planned to drive back to the university at Pietermaritzburg in her mother's Morris Minor, and had promised a lift to a black student called Lewis. On 20 January 1960 she wrote to her mother Margaret Kirwood, who was in charge of the women's hall:

> I have decided on the easiest course for our return to Natal. James will have Lewis with him as far as Umtata. ... From Umtata I am certain that the only disadvantage about possible questioning [by the police about a black man travelling with a white women] is perhaps the nuisance of being held for an hour or two.

In the same letter, Mary vividly described the most remarkable place for parties as being in the home of a Dutchman called Hans Fransen, who lived in a short street of small houses in Wynberg and who corrected proofs for *Die Burger*. He was a Bach addict and one evening started an impromptu concert in the street outside his house with everyone taking part in the cantatas. On one occasion, the former ambassador to London Charles de Water's daughter, clad from masked head to toe in a skin-tight black costume, rode through the party on a black horse. Police watching from the end of the street were found asleep there the next morning.

On another occasion, members of a Muslim Khalifa sect entertained the guests by performing feats such has pushing skewers through their cheeks. Police came but decided to withdraw through a crowd of people patting them on the back with hands – black, white, brown.

'You have arrived at an amusing *time!'*

I was so glad that Randolph used the word 'amusing', for I felt guilty about enjoying all the excitement, even though all sorts of people were having terrible problems. Ralph's journalist friend

Rufus Gibson said he envied me. We were all hoping for a revolution and I felt optimistic that the whole direction of South African history would change soon after I arrived back from a visit to the Eastern Cape. However, despite his 'wind of change' speech to the South African Parliament in February 1960, Macmillan had been wrong in assuming that the South African government was ready for reform. The state was prepared to resort to any means to survive, however violent, and white supremacy was to last for another 30 years.

30,000 Africans march on Cape Town

Since the Defiance Campaign in 1952 against the so-called 'stupid' pass laws, the extra-parliamentary opposition had used non-violent means of protest, but shortly after the Sharpeville massacre took place in the Transvaal in March 1960, there was to be a turning point in South African history.

On 30 March 1960, 30,000 Africans from Nyanga and Langa led by Philip Kgosana, a PAC student wearing shorts, set out for the police station in Caledon Square in Cape Town to offer themselves up for arrest for failing to carry their passes. Kgosana had spent the night before going around the student rooms shouting *'Absolutely no violence! Absolutely no violence!'*

Anthony Millar told me that from his office way up in the BP building, he could see the Africans flooding down the motorway into the centre of town. Apparently, cars with white drivers were having to weave their way through the solid flow of black marchers. The police and army had surrounded Parliament with Saracen armoured cars, so if the 30,000 had headed that way, it might well have produced a massacre far worse than Sharpeville. Instead, the protesters surrounded the police headquarters in Caledon Square in central Cape Town. I was walking through the streets of Cape Town at lunchtime and was totally unaware of this peaceful crowd. Back in the office, Marquard said that he had met the Minister of Bantu Affairs De Wet Nel, who had walked, apparently unguarded, to see the crowd. At 3 o'clock the switchboards jammed as people from the suburbs panicked and rang to tell their partners to come home before rioting broke out – it never did.

Patrick Duncan asked a police officer in Caledon Square how they were going to get the 30,000-strong crowd to disperse, but, apart from resorting to guns, they seemed to have no idea. Patrick discovered that the police had no public address system through which to address the crowd, so having recently stood in the provincial elections in Sea Point, was able to help them rent one. Then, at 6 o'clock that evening, when Kgosana and his colleagues were trying to embark on negotiations about the pass laws, they were arrested. At this point, Marquard exclaimed, 'I don't believe they can have been so stupid!'

Stop it! you police swine! shouts Duncan

Next day the police got their own back in the townships. They also went wild in central Cape Town attacking Africans with homemade rubber coshes. Patrick Duncan, who was in a taxi, shouted at a police officer, 'stop it you swine!', to which he replied, 'this is a state of emergency! We'll lock you up!' A member of the Black Sash stopped her car to see why an African was sitting on the kerb with his feet in the gutter and his head in his hands. He had been walking to the hospital when the police knocked him down. She drove him to hospital and was shouted at by the police who aggressively told her that she should not have done so.

Oh where oh where is Roma?

Basutoland, which was to become independent as Lesotho, was central to South Africa and central to resistance in South Africa. It was on the spine of the Drakensberg, which are mountains of Alpine beauty. With Swaziland and Bechuanaland it made up the High Commission Territories, which had been ruled by Britain.

The Roman Catholic university for the three countries was at Roma in Lesotho. I had met a Wadham South African chemistry lecturer in Cape Town who invited me to visit him and his wife who had been a nurse at the John Radcliffe Hospital in Oxford. It was about thirty miles into the mountains beyond the capital Maseru. A lecturer overheard my frustrated efforts at trying to get through on the telephone. His name was Arthur Jenkins and he gave me careful directions about getting there along mountain roads. 'It is all straightforward except that after the bridge you turn left. Otherwise, you will find yourself arriving at the royal village, the paramount chief of which was at Corpus College in Oxford.'

After the bridge there was a road to the left so I took it. After going up this road through stony drifts(fords) in the setting sun I started to wonder if I was on the right track. I asked a Mosotho in a blanket where the Roma mission was, and he pointed up the valley. When the road deteriorated, I asked another Mosotho in European clothing the way to the university. 'Oh yes!', he said, and I had to go back most of the twenty miles I had taken to find the correct turn. It turns out that I could not have asked a worse question. Every mission church is called Roma because the Roman Catholics rule the territory. If there is a road up a valley there is always a Roma mission.

Police road blocks in the Transkei

The Liberal Party congress was to be in Durban in August 1961. Val Hutchinson, the party secretary, and I shared the driving for the two-day journey in my pale blue Hillman. Randolph had asked me to pick up two people in Umtata, the capital of the Transkei. One of them was the brother of Chief Sabata, with whom Randolph had been doing some work for the

Liberal Party. Once they were safely in the car, we continued to drive towards Natal and Durban. We passed Brokkes Nek near Mount Currie before descending downhill on a long straight road.

At the junction to Kokstad in the far distance, we could see a police Land Rover waiting to stop us. The policeman had written my car registration number on a piece of paper. Unfortunately, one of our passengers had lost his pass, but had reported it missing to the chief magistrate, and the policeman uttered the dreaded words – 'you will have to come along to the charge office.' This certainly meant delay and possible imprisonment for him. I said, 'but surely this is unnecessary officer! He knows his number and has reported the loss!' Luckily, this country policeman was reasonable.

He took our names and addresses and asked whether we knew the whereabouts of a certain car – he gave us the registration number of Randolph's car. Sabata's brother had remembered seeing 'the information officer' near my car, so had presumably taken my number to find out with whom I had been travelling.

We came across another police road block when we stopped for petrol at Umzimkulu near the Natal frontier, and feared that the policeman might be cussed enough to arrest our passenger who was without a pass. Fortunately, at that moment a large American car drew up and a young African got out of it and started boasting that his brother was a chief and with him in the car. We then decided that the best way of getting across to Natal was to segregate the occupants of our cars along colour lines. Consequently, Sabata's brother climbed into the big American car full of black people and went through without being stopped. Our whites only car was also not stopped.

Only white man ever to be executed for a political crime

The Liberal Party congress was in Cape Town in 1963. The best bit was whether there should be a party song and among many suggested were 'Jailhouse Rock' and 'We're Marching to Pretoria'. We had a delegate to stay called John Harris who was terribly fussy about the way Clare made his scrambled eggs. We called him 'Scrambled Eggs Harris'. In 1964 he panicked and exploded a bomb on the concourse of Johannesburg station. He was the only white man in South Africa to be executed for a political crime.

Where were you when you heard that Kennedy had been shot?

On 1 December 1963 we happened to be listening to the 9 o'clock news on vile Radio South Africa and we listened again to the 10 o'clock World Service to have it confirmed.

The interest and passion felt about Kennedy's assassination among Africans and Coloureds was most interesting. 'He was our friend! He would have helped us!' Our maid, Elinor, came in and said that 'do you know that Mr Kenneth the prime minister of England has been shot?' I was pleased to have Kennedy rather than Lord Home attached to my country. Kennedy had the sprightliness of mind and the hard touch of idealism to have got on with sorting out the South African question.

The heresy of multiracialism wins in the Transkei

The result of the Transkei elections of December 1961 was a surprise. The South African United Front standing for the heresy of multiracialism and backed by the Liberal Party did well. The government-backed Chief Matanzima, who took advantage of the government's racism, did less well. This was a triumph for Randolph who, more than anybody else, had enabled some sort of articulation of desires to be made despite the government ban on parties in the Transkei. The chiefs formed an automatic majority in the new assembly. Verwoerd used the British policy of 'divide and rule' to keep white supremacy for a further 30 years.

You really feel that you are in a police state

A bill is going through the assembly to introduce detention without charge for up to twelve days, not just for two days as now. You really feel you are in a police state when you visit a friend – in this case Tom Walters – and find him being escorted out of his third-floor flat by four Special Branch men. I tried to pretend I was going upstairs, but Greef, the nearest Special Branch man to me, asked me what I wanted. I said to Tom, 'I saw your light was on and I came up.' 'Well, I am afraid I am otherwise engaged,' said Tom with a stiff smile.

Around the same time, two other friends had been missing for three days. Tim Holmes and Ibraham Abrahams were arrested while leaving Swaziland on their way back to Cape Town with all their *Contact* equipment in tow. Tim was transferred to Ermelo and the next day to Carolina where he was interrogated by Major van den Berghe, who was specially sent down from Pretoria. Papers were found on Tim about a joke anti-republican demonstration and the police insisted he tell them where he had got them. Fearing that they might impound all the *Contact* equipment, he told the police that the papers had come from Tom Walters.

There was accidental proof that Randolph's telephone was being tapped when an Afrikaner friend of his used it to ring up another friend and the tape recorder accidentally played back the conversation in Afrikaans.

Albie Sachs in solitary

In October 1963 Albie Sachs was kept in solitary confinement with nothing but the Bible to read. He was given only one mug of water to drink. His lawyer asked for him to be given more. The prison authorities said the prisoners were not given bottles because they could smash them and use them as weapons. But in fact it turned out that the bottles were only plastic so prisoners could have them. Albie said that the solitary confinement was the worst aspect of 90-day detention without trial. Some people had been in detention for over 130 days. They were released after 90 days, but many were immediately rearrested – so the bill could be used to keep them indeterminably.

On one occasion, Albie Sachs was released from Roeland Street Prison in central Cape Town and ran down Adderley Street, through to Sea Point and on to Camps Bay where he plunged into the Atlantic in all his clothing. People thought he was trying to escape, but he was just experiencing the joy of freedom. A photograph in one of my books shows Albie on that very beach and Mary Kirwood pouring sand on his back in the shape of a skeleton.

Paperbacks for Africa

In 1961, OUP in London, in association with the Africa Bureau, published a new series of paperbacks called the New Africa Library at two bob a nob (10p).

I waged a personal campaign in OUP Cape Town to get Freddie Cannon's trade department to become more active in distributing the new paperback series to a wider market than just schools. Africans hardly went into bookshops. Tim Holmes, at the liberal newspaper *Contact*, and I thought that an enterprising bookseller should be encouraged to set up a mail-order business with a restricted catalogue of ten or so titles from Penguin, OUP and Pan Books. The bookseller would give a discount to agents. *Contact* had built up a list of agents who made a bit of money for themselves by selling the journal to friends in mine compounds, bus queues and door to door. Marquard said he would put forward the idea to the publisher in London. He said that Cannon was unsure the market existed, but I was certain Cannon did not want to bother to find out if it did. Thomas Nelson was bringing out a series of teach yourself books for Africa, and this was in addition to the Penguin Modern Africa Library and OUPs Three Crowns imprints. Later, a teacher at Waterford School in Swaziland started a mail-order business supplying books that had been banned in South Africa. Each week he read the *Government Gazette*, which gave him a shopping list of the banned books.

Constantia is Vigne country

Liberals worried whether it was politically wise to associate with 'the white tribal parliament' by taking part in the 1961 general election. After much discussion, the Cape Liberals followed the example of the Transvaal and Natal and put Randolph Vigne up as a candidate in Constantia against the United Party, which supported the colour bar. He said 'God! I never expected this to happen to me, or at least not before I became some black man's election agent.'

The Liberal Party used the election to promote non-racial ideas. I spent the afternoon at a polling station and a United Party spokesperson came over to me and said: 'If I were you. I hope you don't mind. It's only friendly advice. But I don't think it does you any good having a native on the table out front.'

A gap in the electoral law in South Africa meant that I could, though not a citizen, go to a magistrate's court to see the verification of postal votes. Councillor Eulalie Stott took Alan Paton, Val Hutchinson and me to see the news editor of the National Party newspaper, *Die Burger*. Alan Paton and he got down to one of those rare Liberal–Nationalist arguments. Alan Paton finished up by saying, 'shall I tell you people how to buy twenty more years in power?' 'You talk of "buy"! Don't morals come into the question?' 'O Yes! as always, but if you want to buy yourselves 20 more years of power put up the wages of the Africans by 50 per cent.' The news editor joked with Paton. 'It's a good thing they took away your passport!'

American visitor arrested for seeing too many Africans

In July 1963 we were asked to take Mrs Calvin Plympton to visit Mavis Orpen and Norah Henshilwood at their home in Kommetjie. Mrs Calvin Plympton was married to the president of Amherst, one of those small expensive American liberal arts colleges.

In September, as she was leaving South Africa, she was arrested at Johannesburg airport and her passport was confiscated from her for 24 hours on the grounds that she had been seeing too many Africans. This was ironic given that a few weeks' later she was scheduled to be the hostess to John F. Kennedy for the opening of a building at Amherst. We trust she told the president all about her South African experiences.

She is a real primitive: primitives are very rare

Tim and I were impressed by the paintings of a Nyanga schoolteacher called Gladys Mgudlandlu and, in 1962, we organised an exhibition of her work in *Contact*'s boardroom. None of the art galleries in town would take her. We invited all the local 'art critics' and were delighted by the enthusiasm of the press. The art critic of *Die Burger* bought one. The SABC reviewed the exhibition and she sold 14 paintings. The artist Cecil Higgs said, 'she is a real primitive! Primitives are very rare!'

In December 1963, 500 people attended the opening of her second exhibition, though the gallery owners only exhibited her sweet and nice pictures.

The vote is not all that important

Where there was money it staggered me. In 1961, for a fat fee, Anglo American mining corporation commissioned OUP to publish a book about them under the title *Sir Ernest Oppenheimer and the Economic Development of Southern Africa*. Anglo American's public relations officer, a Mr Wilson, flew down for the day to discuss the proposal with Leo Marquard and Freddie Cannon. Wilson always referred to Oppenheimer as 'Harry' and Smuts, for whom he had been head of information during the war, as 'the Oubaas'.

Lunch turned into a contest between a Mr Wilson from the Anglo-American mining company and Cannon on the one side of the argument and Marquard and me on the other. At one point, Mr Wilson came up with, 'well, the vote is not all that important', to which Marquard and I chimed in, 'well there is only one answer to that. Why bother to hold it back?' Afterwards, I said to Marquard, 'it hardly feels it is worth bringing up such subjects with such people!' He replied, 'we could not let him get away with that sort of stuff!' Cannon's contribution to the conversation was that 'we ought to bring back flogging because of the crime wave.'

Kidnap and habeas corpus

December 1961 saw a great legal victory against the government. Chief Botha Sicau's home guards had kidnapped a Xhosa political exile named Anderson Ganyile, along with two of his companions, who were from Basutoland and therefore still under British protection. They were then transferred to a prison in Pondoland where, after a whole year of the Transkei being under a state of emergency, people could be held in detention indefinitely.

When Ganyile eventually managed to get a message out of his prison, the Supreme Court, through a writ of habeas corpus, ordered the minister of justice to produce his body alive or dead by 18 January 1962. However, when Benjamin Pogrund, who was at that time deputy editor of the *Rand Daily Mail*, rang the British Embassy in Pretoria to put Patrick Duncan's evidence to it, he was summarily told that 'Mr Duncan's allegations do not warrant serious consideration.'

The kidnapping in Bechuanaland and detention in South Africa of Dr Abrahams and three SWAPO members by South African security forces also resulted in their being released on a writ of habeas corpus. Nonetheless, despite their and Ganyile's case resulting in their release, the British should still have held an inquiry if only to show that there is justice in the High Commission Territories. By September 1963 Patrick Duncan's legal work had begun to bring about some changes.

The South African–Israeli artist Arthur Goldreich, whom police described as the 'arch-conspirator' among those arrested at Rivonia, along with political activist Harold Wolpe and two others, bribed their way out of prison. Goldreich and Wolpe took refuge in Johannesburg's suburbs to evade capture, then escaped to Swaziland concealed in a car boot, and later flew to Botswana in the guise of priests.

I was later to publish a book by Harold Wolpe for UNESCO through my firm, James Currey Publishers.

Africans give English a lift

In June 1961, I attended a discussion focused on what the South African Broadcasting Corporation (SABC) could do about the worsening standard of spoken English. While listening to a whole lot of patronising attitudes about how the Afrikaans language was getting on so well while English was clearly experiencing difficulties, I kept on muttering, 'what about the Africans?' Eventually, Nadine Gordimer swung in with the main reason why she was not worried – it is the Africans who are helping to revivify and revitalise English. She mentioned hearing a young South African at Harvard fluently discoursing with some eminent literary authority. This turned out to be Lewis Nkosi, the young Zulu writer who was at Harvard.

The SA theatre came of age with Athol Fugard's Blood Knot

In February 1962, the production of the *Blood Knot* in Cape Town caused great excitement. Two blood brothers, one white, one dark, talk interminably for three hours in 'waiting for Godot' style. The setting was Wesker – except there was no kitchen sink in their shack. The press proclaimed that South African theatre had come of age in the way that the Australian theatre had come of age in 1955 with Ray Lawler's *Summer of the Seventeenth Doll*. Athol Fugard later became known internationally for his play *The Island* set on Robben Island. He died in 2025.

Sitting it out in the 'sit-ins'

The Johannesburg campaigning magazine, *Drum*, had published an article on the 'sit-ins' in the segregated southern states of America. Then, to follow suit, the Liberal Party decided to organise a 'sit-in' campaign in Cape Town to draw attention to a special proclamation recently gazetted against mixed eating and mixed cinemas.

The Liberal Party informed the newspapers that on a certain Saturday at the height of the morning rush hour, eight or so of its non-white members would go and sit down in the OK Bazaars' tearoom. Although the whole of South Africa was in effect a 'controlled area', the OK Bazaars was not specifically covered by the Group Areas Act. If these eight people were told to leave then thirty or so white Liberals would walk out in protest. When one of the coloured waitresses was about to serve the 60-year-old vice-chairman of the Liberal Party, Mr Cromwell Nododile, the manageress stopped her. There was bit of a discussion and everybody stayed put.

About 15 minutes later, the Special Branch arrived, including its chief, who hung around peering through the racks in the women's dress department. The incident certainly hit the headlines. Journalists from the *Sunday Times, Cape Times, Drum* and *Golden City Post* all gave it between 500 and 1200 words. It was followed the next Saturday with a visit to the poshest store, Stuttafords.

I appeared in a photograph in *The Cape Times* in a delightful, open-air, council-run cafe under the trees in the gardens of the Dutch East India Company. There was no legal colour bar and we wanted to show that people of any colour could go there. We were sitting there under the waving shadows of the trees when I heard the crunch, crunch, crunch of feet on the gravel and thought that this is the heavy brigade coming to beat us up. I spun round and FLASH went the camera of the *Cape Times* photographer. On Monday I was on the front page of *The Cape Times* looking very startled. A week later I was walking along the sand dunes at Hermanus with my Uncle Iver who said: 'Was that you on the front page of the *Cape Times?*' 'Yes,' I said, blushing. 'Don't tell Aunt Iris!' he said.

The difference between a pass and an identity card

The Ovambos came from the frontier area between Angola and South West Africa and there was an Ovambo barber shop on the main road to Sea Point. The Liberal Party was building up an alliance with SWAPO (South West Africa People's Organisation), and its leader in Cape Town was Andreas Shipanga, whose Afrikaans name was Andreas Cloete. He had been educated at an Afrikaner mission and spoke good Afrikaans, so the officials assumed that, though dark black, he must be 'Coloured', namely of mixed race and therefore eligible to apply for an identity card rather than the *dom* pass he had to carry.

He arranged for a photographer friend of his to smear his head and face with margarine and then to photograph him under very strong lighting. This produced such a shine that his photograph for the identity document showed his skin as being considerably lighter than it was. He appeared before the group areas officer whom he addressed humbly in Afrikaans. Although he was standing right there on the other side of the desk for all to see, the official did not look up at him. He merely looked at his photo and stamped his application for an identity card in the name of Andreas Cloete. This legally classified him as 'Coloured'.

FIVE
One Man One Vote

One man one vote

At its congress in April 1960, the Liberal Party was split over whether it should support a progressive franchise or a total franchise. The Progressive Party had broken from the United Party. The young liberals, especially the black members from Natal, said that they could not get Africans to join the only non-racial party unless all its members were treated as equals.

When I first arrived in South Africa, I have to confess that I was in favour of a progressive franchise. In fact, I was deeply shocked when Randolph said that in a few years' time there will be, must be, a black government in South Africa.

President Banda of Malawi remarked that if you do not let Africans practise the vote they will have no chance to learn.

The silent march of ten thousand to the Grand Parade

There were many functions to mark the fiftieth anniversary of the Union of South Africa in 1910. At a meeting dedicated to making a better job of the next fifty years, however, the Liberal Party, along with other opposition groups, organised a march in Cape Town on 5 June 1960.

To the sound of muffled drums we walked up Adderley Street with the sun shining on the backs of our heads. It was so quiet in the surrounding crowds that one could hear individual remarks, like that of a woman saying: 'Why are they looking so sad? I thought they were celebrating Union!'

Eventually, by which time the whole of the Grand Parade was filled with people, our speaker, the former Lord Chief Justice Centlivres, arrived. Although the Black Sash had provided Centlivres with a portable loudspeaker, nobody could hear a word of what he was saying. At that point a Byronic young Liberal Party delegate from Natal offered to read it for him, while he smoked his pipe at the foot of the Boer War memorial.

With the blood of the non-conformist Welsh valleys in his veins, the young delegate made the speech not only audible but also exciting. Cheers and clapping greeted every cliché.

On 19 April 1961 the Liberal Party mounted an Africa Day on the Grand Parade to celebrate the advance of independence in the countries to the north.

Tim Holmes provided his boarding school bed sheets and I painted a giant map of Africa on them. As this sheet map was being carried through the crowd, people threw £70 at it – in cents, pennies and tickies. In fact, the coins rained down quite dangerously onto the back of a lorry that was being used as the platform.

Kicked out of the Commonwealth

There was intense interest in South Africa over whether it would be thrown out of the Commonwealth at the Commonwealth Prime Ministers' Conference of 1961. Verwoerd had shown that he would not move.

When it eventually happened on 6 March 1961, Benny the Coloured liftman announced, 'we've won!' Most Liberals felt it would be better if South Africa were out than in.

Most of the English-speaking South Africans were, however, incandescent with fury. 'O well!' an Englishwoman in the butcher shop said the other day, 'with all those other natives the Commonwealth isn't what it was,' adding that, 'the only difference between now and when Smuts was in power is that the niggers have money.'

'Stay-at-home' equals strike

Since the word 'strike' was illegal in South Africa, during the 50-year celebrations of being a republic, the ANC called for Africans and Coloureds to 'stay-at-home' for three days.

The Minister of Defence announced on 29 April 1961 that the South African Defence Force (which was a militia rather than an army) was to be brought onto a 'war footing'. Anthony Delius wrote in the *Cape Times* that the government 'is arming itself against four-fifths of the inhabitants of the country'. The government in effect banned all parties to the left of the Progressive Party. It seemed determined to create a crisis. It was making it possible to bring out the army without first calling a state of emergency.

We were delivering food parcels because people were not earning. Once, when my car got stuck in the sand, a man pushing beside me mentioned that he had been imprisoned because he had stayed at home, but that he had had to stay at home because he did not have a job to go to and had been arrested.

Patrick Duncan is suppressed as a communist

On 4 April 1961, the Treason Trial was stopped after five years. It indicted 156 people, including Mandela, Tambo and Alex La Guma – the waste of so many valuable people's lives!

Patrick Duncan was banned under the Suppression of Communism Act from attending political meetings consisting of more than two persons. Ironically, he was often accused of defeating the common cause against apartheid by fearlessly showing up the manoeuvrings of the South African Communist Party (SACP) through the pages of *Contact*.

New censorship

In May 1962 some really tough legislation came in. The death sentence was brought in for sabotage (for youths as well as adults). Then the Censorship Act led Patrick Duncan to hand over his editorship of *Contact* to Tim Holmes. The Suppression of Communism Act was extended to cover 'non-communists' such as Patrick Duncan.

Randolph got me to come to the exclusive Kelvin Grove Club to plot. English tribal territory was the best place to discuss plans with Randolph when they were trying to serve a banning order on him.

Election victory in the Transkei

In May 1962 Chief Sabata's party won the Transkei popular election. The chiefs voted to keep the Bunga under the control of Paramount Chief Matanzima. Randolph arranged for the diplomats and journalists to meet the right people. The morning group of newspapers, which includes the *Cape Times*, backed Sabata. After the election Sabata was sent home from Umtata with crowds of Africans celebrating his victory. Meanwhile, Matanzima had to slip shamefully away in the opposite direction in a police car.

Political weekend in the Karoo

In February 1962 we had another Liberal Party weekend at a deserted farmhouse in the Karoo. I was driving a Volkswagen Combi and, as night fell, we found ourselves on the wrong track. We bedded down in the Combi and slept so well that we did not wake up for two hours after sunrise, by which time dassies (rock rabbits) were bouncing around outside our windows.

On the way back, one of our Combis petered out at Touws River with broken bearings. We decided to tow it down to a garage in Worcester. Everybody had to get out and walk on each steep hill. Eventually, the driver of one of our cars went off to ring a garage. To keep ourselves occupied we pushed the Combi up hills and freewheeled down for about five miles. After one hill, which was almost too steep for us and which we only just scaled to the chant of 'One Man One Vote', we stopped, stripped and swam naked in a dam by the side of the road – dipping down when an occasional car came past.

SIX
The New African

The New African *for the new Africa*

We wanted to start a magazine about Africa in general and South Africa in particular and were to have a planning meeting on the afternoon of Saturday 5 July 1961. Nobody could agree about what to call it, but as I mentioned earlier, I had put together four designs for four titles, but was particularly wedded to the *New African*, with its echoes of the left-wing *New Statesman* in London. My design of the headpiece of what Randolph Vigne called 'the clothes hanger men', was immediately accepted. It symbolised that, whatever our colour, we were all Africans living in Africa. Neville Rubin had managed to get money from the Congress for Cultural Freedom in Paris which, it emerged in 1967, was funded by the United States Central Intelligence Agency (CIA).

The Russians were giving away books in Africa, so the CIA-funded Congress in Paris backed such magazines as *Black Orpheus* in Ibadan, *Transition* in Kampala and the *New African* in Cape Town. In July 1962 it ran a Conference of African Writers of English Expression at Makerere University to which Randolph was sent a ticket. He could not go because his passport had been confiscated, so Neville Rubin went and established important contacts across Africa, Britain and America. That meeting was to be central to the establishment of African literature.

The day Natal took off

Anthony Delius wrote a satirical novel in which the National

Party mayor of a dorp, who headed a commission investigating a staggering increase in Immorality Act prosecutions, is caught with a young Zulu woman. Natal secedes.

The book, titled *The Day Natal Took Off*, had already been typeset at the *Cape Times*, but the print manager got a legal opinion and stopped printing because he feared losing government and business contracts. Delius appealed to Randolph and the *New African* took over publication. We would be given the type free and Delius would accept no royalties until money came in. We ordered 3000 copies and immediately sold 2000. Then Pall Mall Press in London ordered 6000. We thought they might be overdoing the South African craze. Colin Legum's review in the *Times Literary Supplement* (TLS) brought enquiries about German, Dutch and Scandinavian rights.

Censorship of the New African *by police raids*

At the beginning of 1964, the Special Branch started harassing the *New African* by means of police raids. Despite the government maintaining that there was a free press, the *Manchester Guardian* reported how the police confiscated all the equipment from the *New African* office. The final filing cabinet was removed by an African worker, followed by a police officer holding an office stamp in front of him as though it were poisonous.

On 18 April 1964, a Special Branch officer visited Len Lee-Warden of Pioneer Press to warn him that if he did not stop printing the *New African* and other political material he would be banned from going into his printing works and would thus be deprived of his livelihood.

Alan Baldwin of the Liberal Party owned a share of a small printing works called Reliance and talked his colleagues into allowing him personally to set the paper after hours and at weekends. We used a different printer for each issue and changed the magazine title, so the government would have to ban each issue. The *New African* had never been prosecuted, yet printers flinched from printing us because the Special Branch would go round threatening to remove their government contracts. The government still maintained that it had a free press.

Contact *office moved to Swaziland to avoid the stay-at-home*

As I mentioned earlier in this book, there had been a three-day 'stay-at-home' to mark the anniversary of the 30,000 march of 1960.

Also, since Patrick Duncan feared that the Special Branch would close down *Contact*, Tim Holmes had agreed to run the journal from the British territory of Swaziland. Patrick asked me if I would take a week's leave from OUP to drive his Volkswagen Combi van, stuffed with *Contact* office equipment, 700 miles to Swaziland where he had made arrangements with a friend to set up the office in a farm outbuilding. Tim would drive direct as he would need his car. The *Contact* worker Ibraham Abrahams, who was classified as a Cape Malay under South African law, was to travel with me, then stay to set up the office.

Over the crest of a hill I hit a sheep at speed and the Volkswagen bumper was driven in against the front tyre. We yanked it out and drove into the nearest dorp to look for a garage, while anxious not to meet the police who might investigate what we were carrying. Suddenly, with a bang, the side of the Combi was dented by a wheel-cap that had spun right across the central reservation from a car undergoing a garage test run. We did a quick deal; in return for leaving the dent, the mechanic would make our bumper safe.

We arrived at the Swaziland frontier after dark and fortunately the customs post was closed. With relief we got beds in the Central Hotel in the capital Mbabane. The manager asked me what nationality my companion was. I said South African. What he meant was what race? He asked us to stay in our bedroom for breakfast. He said 'I'm as against these Nazis as much as you are but some of my regular guests would object.'

Postnatal exercises

Patrick Duncan's friend welcomed us and after the Combi had been unloaded, I set off for the 700-mile journey back to the Cape. I considered sleeping in the van at the roadside, but when in the late evening I saw signs for Klerksdorp, I remembered that fellow Liberal Party members Ferdy and Hélène Nolte were being exiled there for a year while Ferdy, an architect, was rebuilding the Town Hall. Should I ring them? Was it socially permissible to ring them at midnight? Could I beg for a bed? I arrived at one o'clock under the watchful gaze of the police spies in the house opposite. We then talked, drank brandy, and ate scrambled eggs until 3 a.m. They recounted how, during a Special Branch raid on their house the week before, the officer thought he had discovered plans for an English invasion of Natal, but instead came out of the bedroom triumphantly waving a copy of Hélène's postnatal exercises.

A singing school on every hill

Leo Marquard and Alan Paton had fought against the Bantu Education Act of 1953, which was central to bringing apartheid into the school system. However, they decided that OUP could offer African primary schools more appropriate textbooks than their Afrikaner counterparts. Leo had commissioned Edgar Wright to plan and write *The Oxford Course for Bantu Schools* and books for Standards 1–4 had just been printed. I transformed the design of the books for Standards 5–8; in fact, they were the only ones designed for the benefit of teachers. They had been approved by the Bantu Education Department for free supply and were included in the schools' requisition list (but printed illegibly in 8-

point type). My OUP colleagues had done nothing apart from mailing a leaflet. They did not realise that, although the books were free, a promotion job was still required. The large, well-established Afrikaner presses would send former inspectors round so that the schools felt they were being officially informed that they must use books from that particular press.

OUP, along with a couple of its rivals, had got the course approved and put on the requisition list, but this had to be submitted annually by a date in March. Each year, I would choose a different African location township on the edge of a substantial city and visit as many schools in it as I possibly could in a week. Being white, I could see the African principal irrespective of whether or not he was teaching, bring out my copy of the requisition form, show him the entry and leave behind the whole set of textbooks and teachers' books.

One year my visit was to Soweto, the vast township southwest of Johannesburg. Cato Manor outside Durban was the biggest slum in South Africa and built over a cluster of little round hills. On the top of each hill stood a primary school wreathed with singing children. To begin with I used to say how much I enjoyed the singing and the principal would immediately set up a concert. It was delightful, but it slowed my visiting rate. One day I got 29 sets of books into 29 schools in Cato Manor.

My letters give accounts of several marketing tours I made, which gave me more frequent sightings than most white South Africans get of the African locations on the edges of cities that town councils had set up with sub-standard housing and minimal schools.

Vast journeys on national roads

I never was able to travel by the magnificent South African Railways. The steam locomotives were still coal burning. I promised to collect two teenage cousins after travelling at the end of term to Cape Town from Grahamstown. The 'white' children were coloured bronze with smoke. Since coming to power in 1948 the National Party government had transformed the network of national roads. It was not mentioned that of course they were also planned for military movement to suppress any resistance.

I made multiple use of these vast journeys, sometimes of up to 700 miles in a day. The business paid for the car and accommodation and lots of the authors, academics and booksellers I visited for OUP became friends and invited me to stay. I would especially enjoy organising visits to the British High Commission Territories of Basutoland, Bechuanaland and Swaziland, where many political activists were in exile.

One such activist was Collingwood August, who had been the assistant editor of *Contact* but now lived in exile in Leribe in Basutoland, 60 miles from the capital Maseru. He was glad of my company one moonlit night when we went round to a priest's house. We were drinking the communion wine when there was a knock on the door – the police! It was an enormous Basotho mounted policeman who, as soon as he found out I was English, wanted to talk about his time at the police college in Hendon. Collingwood conjectured that when he saw my Cape Town plates he would have wondered if I was into illicit diamond buying (IDB).

When the UN Globemasters roar south

Patrick Duncan mounted an expensive campaign in America to try to persuade the United Nations to invade and overthrow the South African government. The UN already provided an army in pale blue berets for the former Belgian Congo.

After one of his secret trips through Africa, Patrick Duncan took us into his loft – it was less likely than elsewhere in his house to have been bugged – to tell us where he had been in Africa and America and what he had been doing for the last six months. At the conclusion of his briefing, he excitedly exclaimed: 'when the Globemasters roar south!' For the uninitiated, Globemasters are vast transport planes that are capable of carrying tanks and bridges.

On my way to that meeting, just as I was leaving De Waal Drive and heading towards Patrick's house, I was stopped by the police. I feared that they might have known that I was going to a secret meeting, so it was a great relief to discover that my only penalty was to be a fine for speeding.

SEVEN

A Swing through West Africa

July 1962: A swing through West Africa

My travel agent had pointed out that a BOAC ticket enabled me to stop off wherever I wanted on my way back to Britain for my five months' leave. To take advantage of this opportunity, I therefore secured invitations to visit the OUP offices in Salisbury in Rhodesia. I also arranged visits to Lagos and Ibadan in Nigeria, and to Accra in Ghana, as well as stop-offs in Douala and Victoria in Cameroun and Dakar in Senegal.

I even went to Conakry. Guinea had become isolated because it was the only francophone country that had dared vote '*non*' in the independence referendum to a continued association with France. Russia, which had donated little to it in foreign aid, thought it could step in and dump millions of bidets without any plumbing. In Guinea, the Reuters correspondent – the only other guest in the Hôtel de France – took me to see that notorious sight.

Five months to get Clare to marry me

Having been in Cape Town since July 1959, I arrived back in Britain in July 1962 determined to use the five months of my leave to persuade Clare to marry me and to get her to come back for the second half of my OUP contract in Cape Town. I had as allies her parents Ruth and Henry Wilson – her father was a former Harley Street psychiatrist. When I told my mother that we were thinking of getting married, she said: 'She will never let you down.' She nearly did. She was devoted to her job in the Department of Aerial

Photography at the University of Cambridge. Her boss St Joseph, although married, then declared his love for her. Clare said, 'I think I love St Jo more than you.'

When I was assembling *From Sharpeville to Rivonia*, I asked Clare for my letters. She said she had felt so let down by somebody called Peter that she had decided she was 'finished with men' and had destroyed all her letters from men friends. There is a sole letter from me to Clare dated 25 May 1960 saying, 'how nice to get a happy bouncing letter from you full of freedom from Rowntree's cocoa.' After Oxford she had got a job at Rowntree's, her family firm in York, but had found it lonely, so when her parents moved from London to Cambridge, she joined them there.

Ruth and Henry Wilson, on taking us for a walk on the Gog Magog Hills, were delighted to see how happy we were to be with one another again. At the end of October, I collected a new red Volkswagen Beetle from Dusseldorf and drove to her thatched cottage in Cottered and proposed to her.

Gabrielle Chavasse gave us an engagement party in South Audley Street. Clare asked about an engagement ring and I said that she had not accepted my proposal. So, in Piccadilly, on the way to the party, for ten shillings I bought her a ring with an enormous chunk of coloured glass, which she could flash at the party.

Would Clare call the wedding off?

I drove to Southampton at the beginning of Christmas week to put the Beetle on the Union Castle boat to Cape Town. I rang her from a press-button-B telephone box; I stumbled out of the phone box convinced she was going to call off the marriage before the very next Friday, Midwinter's Day. On the afternoon of 21 December 1962, I married Catherine Clare Wilson. She continued to be filled with doubts; as she was driving to the wedding at the Friends Meeting House in Cambridge, her very Quaker mother said, 'well dear! you could always get divorced!'

Clare and Ruth Wilson arrive at Friends' Meeting House for our marriage in Cambridge on 21 December 1962.

Clare and James cut their wedding cake at the reception at Emmanuel College, Cambridge after their marriage.

To get married we stood, held hands, and each said to one another, 'I take thee my friend …' Clare was wearing a superb green velvet dress and white muff. Stella had wanted her father, the Revd J. P. Martin, to marry us. The Methodists are masters of extempore prayer, so I asked him to make his contribution whenever the spirit moved him. It was indeed a moving prayer. He had said to me that he admired the Quakers; 'But they don't shout enough for me.' We got married on Midwinter's Day, 21 December 1962. Together, we visited both our families over Christmas.

EIGHT
With Clare to the Cape

Arrival with Clare in Cape Town

Our flight from Heathrow was delayed by snow falling and it would remain on the ground in Britain all that winter. The airline put us up in Athens. A Labour MP on the flight asked if we had just got married. He said he guessed so because I had asked Clare what drink she wanted on the plane.

We stayed in Cairo in the Hotel Cosmopolitan, which had pot plants in the lifts for spies such as Philby to plot behind. Flying up the Nile Valley gave us a sight of the watered valley stopping at the rigid line of desert.

For New Year 1963 we stayed with OUP friends in Nairobi and Clare took a picture of lions with factories in the background. On 2 January 1963 we arrived in Cape Town. Anthony and Joy Millar had kept my flat vacant during my leave and delightedly welcomed Clare.

Views of Table Mountain and Table Bay

Randolph found us an architect-designed first-floor flat complete with built in desk and a fireplace and with woods on the other side of the road. From the balcony it had Table Mountain on one side and views across the city, the docks and the bay on the other. The memorable address was 101 Kloof Nek Road.

Clare set out to look for a job. She started with an agency for temporaries; one job was with an advertising agency making films. She found a job teaching Latin to spoilt rich kids in Cape Town's

The first floor flat at 101 Kloof Nek Road.

The built in desk and bookshelves.

poshest prep school and was sacked. Fortunately, a Quaker academic at the University of Cape Town was finishing a book on cancer in Cape Town and needed an editor. Muire Grieve was doing pioneering work on how different skin colours influenced the onset of cancer. She had an office looking out onto zebras. In compensation for all Clare's doubts about marrying me and leaving family and friends, Clare's parents were to come to visit us at the end of 1963, complete with their Morris Minor convertible.

Clare wrote to her parents on 10 January 1963 saying that Norah Henshilwood, former head of the leading teacher's college had straight away taken her to the Black Sash advice centre so she could see how the Africans had to carry 'the stupid (*dom*) pass'. Mavis Orpen lived with Norah at Kommetjie some 30 miles from Cape Town in a house overlooking the beach; they had an open invitation to our network of friends to come for lunch on any Sunday. Clare could confide in Mavis.

Clare sees Randolph banned

On 21 February 1963 Alan Paton, author of *Cry, the Beloved Country*, was to speak at the Claremont Hall to protest against the new wave of banning orders against Liberals. When the Special Branch arrived to place Randolph under a banning order, he had managed to escape from his back door and disappear up Lion's Head. He then spent some 15 days taking a last chance to visit his network across the country, but decided that, to achieve maximum publicity, he should break cover at Paton's meeting.

Two weedy members of the Special Branch took him outside the hall to issue him with his banning papers. Although there were a few hisses, the Special Branch officers were surprised by the lack of protest, so I yelled 'three cheers for Randolph!' and then a great roar went up from the crowd. Gillian Vigne was in the lavatory, which led Clare to make a ditty: 'O dear, what can the matter be, Randolph's wife is locked in the lavatory.'

James and Clare above Hout Bay.

Clare had doubts about whether, as a foreigner, she should join the Liberal Party, but now felt she must. As usual, she stood out in the press photographs.

I ban you here and I ban you there

Clare had her first experience of a Liberal weekend summer school in February 1963. A remote farm house at the end of a sandy track reached over two mountain ranges. There was no sanitation and water had to be collected from a spring. I gave a talk for an hour and forty minutes about my recent visit to newly independent colonies in West Africa, followed by a great braaivleis with chops grilled over an open fire. There were toasts and songs such as 'Old Verwoerd had a farm with "I ban you here" and "I ban you there!"' And Minister De Wet Nel with 'a Ban-tustan here and a Ban-tustan there'.

NINE
The 90-Day Police State

Alan Paton, at a meeting on 26 April 1963, made the following announcement: 'I said a couple of years ago that South Africa is not a police state, but a good imitation of one. I should like to withdraw that statement [the Special Branch man scribbled hard] … and replace it with "South Africa is about to become a police state."' Any policeman without a warrant could now put anybody in prison for 90 days and then rearrest the same person for a further 90 days ad infinitum.

While driving along in the arid Karoo one Saturday, passing nothing but an occasional klipspringer and lone Cape cart, we suddenly came over a rise and lo and behold a new prison was under construction. At that time, the convict labourers were playing football behind the fence. The 90-day state needed prisons.

'You've got to let the Bantu talk'

In May 1963, while driving from East London to Pietermaritzburg I stopped off in Umtata at 10.00 a.m. to visit three schools. I also went to the Bunga (the Transkei parliament) where I bumped into the press reporter Hugh Lewin. Hugh had just asked the deputy minister of Bantu affairs why the whole proclamation about who could vote in the bantustans had been rushed through to a vote before lunch. Hugh questioned whether, since it had already gone through the Cape Town Parliament, the morning's debate in the Bunga would make any difference. The deputy minister's reply was that 'you have got to let the Bantu talk.'

Randolph's trials

In February 1964 Randolph was charged with contravening his banning order by visiting the Transkei. The case in Umtata was postponed so that a handwriting expert could compare two sets of handwriting. In May, to everybody's amazement, the magistrate rather impatiently dismissed the case. To all intents and purposes, Randolph was as guilty as anything, but the prosecution had apparently lied about everything. ('So of course did we!' said Randolph.)

A heated debate with Muslims

Roger Wilson, a Quaker relation of Clare's and a professor of education at Bristol, visited Cape Town in April 1984. This was immediately after he had been working in Kinshasa for a year at the height of the Congo crisis. He addressed a meeting of young Cape Town Muslims, of which several of the more militant ones attacked him for being an apologist for Britain, an apologist for Christians, an apologist for whites and an apologist for the United Nations. They were certain that the UN had organised Lumumba's murder. Roger had been president of the students' union in 1929, the most prestigious position for an undergraduate at Oxford, and you could see him enjoying calling on all his old debating skills. (His brother Geoffrey Wilson was president of the union in 1931.)

Learning the mindset of escape

In April 1964 a Cape Town Quaker, Carl Ohland spoke about his wartime escape from Germany to Denmark. He had deserted from the German army on the Russian front and decided he must get across the border to Denmark in an attempt to reach Sweden.

At the border all the soldiers had to descend from the train and queue down a corridor to have their papers checked by one or other of the two border guards sitting at two desks.

He thought that, given his papers, he had little chance of getting through. Fortuitously, the soldier standing behind him rather rudely pushed him out of the way and he found himself standing between the two guards at the two desks. On realising that he had been shoved into no-man's land, he brazenly walked past the second guard hoping that he would assume that the first guard had checked his papers.

His ploy had worked and he was now in Denmark where he somehow managed to get in touch with the Danish underground. One night shortly thereafter, he was rowed out of Copenhagen harbour and across to Sweden. What he told us about handling danger and calmly just taking things as they came was to influence my mindset during my own Cape escape only three months later.

TEN
Husbands in the Dock

Dread Pretoria for the Rivonia Trial

On 16/17 April 1964 I was visiting schools in Soweto (the Southwestern Townships) and Clare got a lift from Johannesburg to Pretoria to attend the Rivonia Trial of the African National Congress (ANC) leadership. She wrote a piece called 'Rivonia Notebook', which she published under the pseudonym Elizabeth Wilson in the *New African* on 6 June 1964. It movingly conveyed the atmosphere: 'you think you recognise Mrs Mandela and perhaps Mrs Sisulu and wonder how you would feel if it were your husband facing the judge. If you knew he faced sentence of death, would you be able to bear being there day after day; would you be able to bear not being there?'

My leap from the *Thorstream* three months later was only five fingers from disaster. Clare and Gillian might have had every day to watch Randolph and me on trial – Randolph for his life.

Down a cracky road

We published a vivid article in the *New African* (21 September 1963) called 'In a dim world: the compound is a meerkat burrow'. It was written by a Jacob Mokholo under the pseudonym Carl Mafoko, and Randolph and I were particularly struck by it. Jacob Mokholo's address was a P.O. Box number in Pietersburg, which is on the road north to the frontier post with Southern Rhodesia at Beit Bridge. He sent us directions about how to get to him. These instructions gave no idea of distance, only of direction. At

HUSBANDS IN THE DOCK

Jacob Mokholo wrote vivid stories for The New African. *We made an 80-mile detour down a 'cracky' road to his Venda village. The Special Branch raided that night. BOSS (Bureau of State Security) files record that they followed us for all of the three weeks of our visit to friends in the British colonies of Zambia, Malawi, Rhodesia, and Swaziland.*

Bochum post office we were to go south past the Devonia rolling mills and turn off for the village of Terbrugge. We were to ask at any African store where Jacob Mokholo's house was and were told that we would 'find it down a cracky road'. We had been involved in many wild goose chases in the Cape. This venture into the bushveld seemed fraught with the danger of never getting to our target. When we did reach Terbrugge a young chap tore up on a bicycle and stopped. I said 'Do you know Jacob Mokholo?' 'Yes! I am Jacob Mokholo!'

After about three miles we got to his parents' house, which consisted of five rondavels grouped round a courtyard made of cement and cow dung. Joining the rondavels was a wall with designs in ochre; Venda wall decorations are renowned. Three little black pigs, very neat and clean, were snuffling around. I encouraged him to send any work to me at OUP. He had started a novel in Nothern Sotho. He said he thought only educated people could write and that he could not understand why his teachers were not writing books. He only had a few books – a couple of Jane Austens, a Conrad, a George Eliot, a couple of Dickens. There was no library for Africans closer than Pretoria.

The detour added about eighty miles to our journey, but how glad we were to have taken it. However, we had been naive to have undertaken such a visit. The Special Branch came that night and interrogated him. We had not thought we were important enough to be worth watching. The Bureau of State Security (BOSS) followed us right through the British colonies – Southern Rhodesia, Northern Rhodesia, Malawi and Swaziland. The assumption was that we were using the cover of Oxford University Press to carry messages for the African Resistance Movement (ARM). We were just visiting friends. At that time we did not even know of the ARM.

Kruschev, Nikita and Keeler, Christine

At Beit Bridge the South African officials were dour and the Rhodesian officials treated the whole operation with cheerful contempt. They had filled in sample immigration forms for Kruschev, Nikita and Keeler, Christine. Maybe even for Marx, Groucho and Marx, Karl. They gave you smart salutes under their wide-awake brims as you crossed the bridge and entered Rhodesia.

After dark we reached the rest camp at the Victoria Falls, where you can hire a rondavel for a few shillings. They have little cooking huts with old ranges stamped 'Welcome – Dover'. There was an affable servant who did our washing up. He was most disappointed by our lack of children. He said 'I make four. I want to make twelve – if I am good!'

ELEVEN
Great Trek to Central Africa

Clare and James's 'great trek' to Central Africa

In 1964, Clare and I set off from Cape Town in our little red Volkswagen Beetle to visit the three countries to the north of South Africa. The car, which had been newly bought from Dusseldorf when I drove it to Cottered determined to propose to Clare, was to reach the northernmost turning point of this particular trek at the Victoria Falls in Southern Rhodesia, which was then still a British colony.

At this time Northern Rhodesia was due to become Zambia in October. In Lusaka, we stayed with Tim and Sally Holmes, friends from Cape Town who were teaching at Munali School, which was where practically all the members of the first Zambian cabinet had been educated.

From Salisbury, we flew to Nyasaland where we stayed with Clare's cousins Anne and Anthony Wilson. They were both working for the Department of Community Development to help train people in local government for when the country was to become Malawi in July. Clare's photograph of the Independence Office appeared on the cover of the *New African* on 11 July 1964, the day we were to flee from South Africa. The Bureau of State Security (BOSS) files in Pretoria has all our visits to the British colonies on record. It was keeping its eye on the *New African*.

Clare and I disliked Southern Rhodesia where racism was more crudely in evidence than in South Africa. The OUP manager took us to some English-style horse trials and shouted at the 'munt' ice cream seller every time he came past, when he was only doing his job. At one time OUP had apparently been considering me, for the second part of my contract, to take over the Salisbury office from David Philip. Since that would have involved marketing rather than editorial work, it was fortunate for me that Marquard wanted to keep me in Cape Town to work with him alongside David Philip.

The Great Zimbabwe ruins and the politics of race

It is interesting how white southern Africans react to the Great Zimbabwe ruins, for they mostly deny that the indigenous people could have built them. Although my Aunt Iris described them as 'out of this world', she and others like her tend to prefer the works of the Phoenicians, Arabs or Portuguese. Nobody, however, can deny that the vast Zimbabwe ruins are remarkable given that these people built the dry stone walls without mortar and cement, did not use measuring rods and had no idea of simple geometry. The buildings are also extraordinary with respect to the sheer volume of stone that had been transported to the site. These are perhaps the most remarkable buildings I have seen in Africa and archaeological evidence seems to point to the superiority of African builders. Clare's experience at the Cambridge University's Department of Aerial Photography of working for distinguished archaeologists meant that she was able to give me many exciting insights as we went round.

TWELVE
James Leaps off Thorstream

I leap off Thorstream *to enable Randolph to escape to Canada*

Randolph was in Port Elizabeth when he went to the airport to buy a copy of the Johannesburg *Sunday Times*, and read of the arrest of Adrian Leftwich. After driving back to Cape Town with Norman Bromberger, he decided not to sleep at Clifton House. Instead, under a false name I booked him into a Sea Point hotel for several nights, and he took the precaution of using the back stairs to reach his room. He spent the days at Jean Ridge's photographic studio. He felt certain he had to get out of South Africa and various options were considered.

I suggested he and I swap our Volkswagen Beetles and he drive to Bechuanaland. A friend of his called Bill Bowater had always said he could use his British passport to buy a last-minute ticket and travel under his name, but that was impractical because he was out at Paarl.

Then Jan Aase, the Norwegian consul, mentioned that on the afternoon of Friday 9 July a Norwegian freighter called *Thorstream* would be leaving for Canada and that a cabin had become available. Clare immediately agreed that since Randolph and Gillian were our friends, we must help them, so I went round to its agents, the Holland-Afrika Line, to buy the ticket. When signing the papers needed to leave South Africa and enter Canada I said I would be visiting the OUP office in Toronto.

Towards 5 o'clock Jean Ridge, Randolph Vigne and I walked up the gangplank at the stern of the ship and went to the cabin booked for me. To our amazement, Jean Ridge had established that there was no need for me to show my passport. However, when we headed to the gangplank to leave the ship, we noticed that the Holland-Afrika agent was watching the last of the visitors leaving the ship. He would surely recognise me!

The ever resourceful Jean said 'leave this to me!' I ducked in a crew member's cabin but thought it looked as if I were a stowaway. I emerged to find that Jean Ridge had managed to charm the Holland-Afrika man away from the gangplank. However, at that point he saw me on deck looking anxious and asked Jean if everything was all right. This broke Jean Ridge's powers of distraction and he turned back to the gangplank.

I had seen that the ship deck was riding about six feet higher than the quay and about six foot away from it. I swung my legs over the railing and jumped. After banging my shin on the wooden edge of the quay, I realised that I would land closer to the water than the wharf. I pictured myself being pulled out of the sea in a dripping winter suit and all being revealed. I saved myself with the fingers of one hand and pulled myself frantically up onto the quay. A passenger screamed but apparently the Holland-Afrika agent did not turn round to see what was happening.

Jean started running to her car and I said, 'we must walk! We must walk!' Jean drove like mad until we were behind the cooling sheds but approached the harbour gates slowly. There she smiled at the officer and asked him in Afrikaans if it were all right to go through. In the mass of crossroads the driver of another car and she engaged in elaborate 'after you' and 'after you' signs. I asked who the man was and she said 'my former husband!'

Peter Hjul, the chairman of the Cape Liberal Party, was editor of *Shipping and Fishing News* and therefore had constant professional dealings with the immigration officer in the Sanlam building, which towered above the foreshore. Afterwards, he was able to tell us what had happened. The Holland-Afrika office would have immediately sent my papers to him by messenger. Randolph and I had the amazing good fortune that the immigration official had scarpered off early to go away with his family on a national holiday weekend. He would surely have spotted that I, as a Liberal activist, was leaving South Africa in a suspicious rush. By the time he saw the papers on his desk, the *Thorstream* would have been out of South African waters and Clare and I would have been in London. When the *Thorstream* came back from Canada the Special Branch would swarm in frustration all over the ship.

THIRTEEN
Escape from South Africa

The British consul says 'get out quick.'

The British consul advised me to leave South Africa before the Norwegian *Thorstream* reached Montreal. I told him that, since the Canadians would let him ashore I would continue to work in South Africa. He offered to come with me to see Cannon and to point out to him that he would not want to have OUP's name in the papers if I were to be arrested. The consul told me that he believed that I did not know what Vigne had done. However, if the police arrested me they certainly would not believe me and their interrogation would be merciless. The sooner I got out of South Africa the better. If I got arrested he would do his best to get me expelled. The British consul made it clear that he was acting for me and not for Vigne. He was concerned about my safety as a British citizen.

On Friday afternoon I told Fred Cannon, the trade manager of Oxford University Press, how I had enabled Randolph Vigne to escape and that I had booked seats on an Alitalia flight on Saturday on which Clare and I would fly from Cape Town to Johannesburg and then onwards to London. Cannon went bright red and said, 'you mean to say…' and then stopped because the British consul was there. The story – simple and straightforward – was that my mother was dangerously ill.

At Cape Town airport I retired to the lavatory. The announcements were first in Afrikaans and then in English. Then there was an announcement asking 'passenger Kerry' to go to the flight desk. Afrikaners often mispronounced my name as 'Kerry'. I said to Clare as I passed, 'this sounds like it!' To my relief, there was another passenger called Kerry, so I returned to the lavatory.

We waited nervously at Johannesburg's Jan Smuts Airport for the connecting flight. As it was a Saturday, we had the home number of the British consul – James Currie! – and Clare had a tickey coin for the push coin phone box. Again, I went to hide in the lavatory. The Alitalia Flight in from Rome was three hours late. The sun was going down as the plane headed for Kinshasa in the Congo and we were given an airline lunch to eat. It tasted so good. Half way to Kinshasa we thought that, if the plane had problems, it would not turn back to Johannesburg. We began to allow ourselves to think that we had escaped.

We were too late for the connecting flight for London so Alitalia put us up for the night in the honeymoon suite of a hotel in Rome. We had no money, so insisted that Alitalia cable the Wilsons with the time of our afternoon arrival at Heathrow. Not surprisingly, both the Wilsons and Curreys were there to meet us. Indeed, Nick Elam, the son of the CRGS headmaster, was on the South African desk at the Foreign Office in London and could tell Ralph and Stella about every stage of our flight once we had got out of South Africa. The Wilsons had managed to borrow a flat for the night from friends near Regent's Park, which meant that we could stay overnight before I went on Monday morning to report to the OUP office in London.

'You could not have done otherwise! Can't think what job we've got'

On Monday morning I was on the steps of OUP's elegant Amen House near St Paul's. I first saw the publisher John Brown, who was the managing director of a limited liability company. He had started in the Indian branch. This meant that he, like people in the Indian Civil Service, assumed an arrogant superiority. It was therefore fortunate that I was able to say that Randolph Vigne was working in the publishing business, and a relief that I did not seem to have been sacked.

I then saw Philip Chester, a deputy publisher and friend of my father's who said, 'accidents happen. You might have been run over by a bus. It may be a bit of time before we can find a job for you.' David Neal, the overseas manager with whom I had got on well during his recent visit to Cape Town, took a drag on his fag and said gruffly, 'you could not have done otherwise! Can't think what job we've got. Better take three weeks leave while we find something.' To Rex Collings, the publisher of the Three Crowns series of new writing from across the world, I was a hero.

Disgracey

My last business trip before leaving South Africa had been to King William's Town to train our new Xhosa traveller who was to build up sales in the first bantustans of Ciskei and Transkei. Over our last breakfast the traveller mentioned that he knew the director of education in the Transkei, so I asked him to ring him and fix an appointment that afternoon for 3 o'clock.

We just made it in time on rough country roads and had a most positive meeting. OUP sales rose after the establishment of the bantustans because their nominal independence allowed them to reject the courses that former inspectors had written for the Afrikaner presses. In a recent (2022) book by Caroline Davis of Oxford Brookes University, the credit for this was improperly given to Gracey rather than to David Philip.

When Marquard retired, OUP in London should have made David Philip its next Cape Town manager. Instead, it chose a bookseller called Gracey who, it turned out, had not only worked for the National Party but had also been convicted of distributing pornography from his Durban bookshop.

David Philip sent a press cutting about Gracey to the London office, but by deciding against withdrawing Gracey's appointment, made it impossible for David Philip to remain in the firm. Gracey later used the OUP stockroom in Cape Town to return to his illegal

Marie Philip at lunch with Eddie Daniels. Eddie Daniels spent 15 years on Robben Island in 'B Section' in the company of Mandela and Sisulu. Facing a possible death sentence he refused to turn state witness.

activity. Jon Stallworthy, my renowned contemporary who became a professor of English at Oxford, did everything he could to get OUP to cancel Gracey's appointment, but to no avail. I named him 'Disgracey'. Fortunately, David and Marie Philip went on to set up their own publishing firm, which eclipsed OUP.

Where would we find to live in England?

When we unexpectedly arrived home, Ralph and Stella were about to set off to visit Aunt Joan and her recently acquired husband. He was Harold Culver, a retired professor of geology known as 'old hickory', and he took them on a tour of every rock in Washington State and Vermont. They were thus able to allow us to have 3 Beverley Road, Colchester to ourselves, which was only an hour by train to Liverpool Street and OUP.

Clare's parents in Cambridge then kindly looked after us in

their elegant former farmhouse just across the river on the higher ground above what is now the Kettle's Yard museum. One of Clare's doubts about marrying me and going to South Africa was because she found her job at the Cambridge University Department of Aerial Photography so fulfilling. The department was glad to have her back working for a few weeks helping the person who took over from her how to use Ordnance Survey maps to locate various historical sites.

Clare pressed me to use my train commutes from Cambridge to London and back to jot down my memories of our escape from the Cape. Those handwritten notes were later to prove valuable when I was writing the revised version of *The New African: A History*, which was to included a substantial section on my escape from the Cape.

Our return had been a surprise for the Whites, our former Cape Town colleagues who were renting Clare's thatched cottage at Cottered in rural Hertfordshire. They agreed to leave in October, so in September we went on holiday to Dublin and Clifden – rain-soaked bogs sinking into the Atlantic! While the cottage was within reach of Stevenage station, I was yet to find out how difficult it might be to commute daily to Oxford University Press near St Paul's.

James and Clare as a team

Clare and I delighted in working problems out together, but it was almost always Clare who had the inspiration. After we had escaped from South Africa we worked together on a succession of projects. Clare imagined the possibilities of Walkern Mill. She inspired me into starting James Currey Publishers and we faced up to the dangers that working together would pose for our marriage.

Clare did not like London and we researched moving from Islington; we thought of Edinburgh, York, Cambridge or Oxford. Fortunately, Douglas Johnson, our new partner, lived in Oxford. His wife Wendy James, a professor of anthropology, found a house in Botley Road. The James Currey office was set up on the ground floor with our flat above where we could live during the working week.

Clare realised that we needed to have our own house and decided to look near Folly Bridge. She found No 72 Thames Street, which faced south-west over the river. It was in a distressed state as it had been camped in by students. Hal was delighted by the opportunities it gave him as an architect. He added on a studio extension a few years later, which, with its bathroom, was useful when Clare was confined to bed and when I was hampered in my walking.

Clare had to make an offer for No 72 when she had three invalids to care for. I was going into hospital to have my hip replaced in Oxford, my father was seriously ill in Colchester, and our horse in Hertfordshire had laminitis.

I take over Three Crowns from Rex Collings

David Neal found me an editorial job and an office in the Overseas Education Department proof-reading textbooks and academic books on Africa. I was relieved to have a job and it was sensible not to be under much pressure. Rex Collings had started the Three Crowns series in 1962 to publish literary work from the Third World. The Mbari Club in Ibadan produced plays and poetry written predominantly by Leeds graduates Wole Soyinka and J. P. Clark. Rex Collings subcontracted the Mbari plays for a world market. Oxford University Press had a self-denying ordinance against publishing novels that were to be central to the success of Heinemann's African Writers Series.

Rex Collings said to me in January 1965, 'I am going to tell you something I am not telling anybody else in OUP. I have been offered a job in three months at Methuen's on condition I take Wole Soyinka with me! They have one of the three best drama lists in London. When I leave, you are the only person they have available to offer my job to.' I inherited his enormous six-foot green tin cupboard stuffed full of manuscripts by the new wave of young African writers.

Soon afterwards, Oxford University Press moved us all from Amen House to Ely House, a grand West End office with marble halls and an eighteenth-century frontage that stretched to the next street. In Edwardian times, it had been converted into the Albemarle Ladies Club. Mary Dyson and I had facing desks in the same office and were to become lifelong friends.

By chance, the Transcription Centre run by Dennis Duerden, formerly of the BBC Hausa Service, was in the house next door. It recorded transcriptions of talks with African writers and sent them out to the newly created postcolonial radio stations that provided national broadcast alternatives to the BBC World Service.

It was an important patron for London-based young writers, several of whom had been published by Rex Collings in Oxford's Three Crowns series. Lewis Nkosi, journalist, poet, playwright, found much work at the Transcription Centre and edited a cultural newsletter. I often took sandwiches round at lunch time and met up between recording sessions with writers, artists and academics on their way between Africa and America.

Don't have South Africa on our child's passport

Within days of our trip home in July, Clare calmly said that we should have a baby and Hal arrived within ten months on 27 April 1965. Clare perceptively said she did not want 'South Africa' as the place of birth on her child's passport. Her mother Ruth decided the baby would not be born at Paddocks Wells in Hertfordshire but at their home in Mount Pleasant, Cambridge; if anything went wrong, Addenbrooke's was nearby.

Clare's father, who was a retired consultant psychiatrist, was sent elsewhere to stay with family. Ruth brought Miss Nattriss, the nurse for her three children, out of retirement. It had become the

Henry and Ruth Wilson's house Mount Pleasant in Cambridge where both Hal and Tamsin were born.

fashion that the young father should be actively involved and helpful at the birth. Clare knew how nervous I was of the fearsome demands of childbirth. On the morning of 27 April 1965 Hal was on his way. The midwife left Clare at about 10 a.m. saying that the birth would not be for a bit and that the doctor was coming. Suddenly at 10.15 a.m. everything was happening and I leapt downstairs to ring the doctor and while I was phoning Hal arrived. So, to my great relief, I missed the birth.

Jon Stallworthy, who was a poet, was also a colleague of mine at OUP and it turned out that Jill was expecting their first child at the same time as Clare. Jon and I regularly exchanged news as expectant fathers and I passed on reports to Clare.

Jon's father, who was on the way to becoming professor of obstetrics at Oxford, went to see his newly arrived grandson and immediately suspected Down's Syndrome. Clare, just before the birth of Hal, asked me whether the Stallworthy baby was a boy or girl and, as I did not want to tell her, I said I did not know. Clare said about me, 'typical man!'

J. P. Martin, author of Uncle the Elephant, *and his first great-grandson Hal in their deck chairs.*

A tendency to faint

I have always had a tendency to faint. I picked up a tapeworm while in South Africa. For its easy removal I was summoned into the Hospital for Tropical Diseases in St Pancras because, after a weekend of starvation, on Monday morning it was scheduled to be poisoned by feeding it on a male fern. I was in the next bed to an actor who had been on a production shoot in Thailand for Conrad's *Lord Jim*. On the Sunday evening we were in the common room watching a film when I was summoned out by the sister so that she could run me through the medical procedure for Monday morning; I fainted onto the ground. My *Lord Jim* friend was watching on television the body of Charles Laughton being carted off screen when he heard the crash outside, rushed out and, seeing my body on the floor, exclaimed, 'Is he dead? Is James dead?'

Then, on another occasion, I was at Paddocks Wells where there were steep stairs down to the room where Hal was in a cot. Hal started crying in the early hours one night. I leapt out of bed, rushed downstairs, fainted over the cot and crashed to the ground. Clare guided me back up the stairs to bed. I lay on my back frantically feeling my chest saying, 'have I had a heart attack?' Clare said forthrightly, 'No! It would jolly well hurt if you had had a heart attack.' One time, when Clare was lying in bed expecting a miscarriage and the doctor was telling her what would happen, I sank to the floor in a faint. The doctor said to Clare, 'does he do this often?'

Come on, Tamsin!

Fortunately, Clare never miscarried again and Tamsin was expected in August 1967, but inconveniently, like me, was not arriving before the beginning of the new school exam year in September. We tried various things to bring on her birth. Sister-in-law Jane recommended cherry brandy. Clare and I set off in the Beetle to encourage her to arrive by bouncing over the tracks at the building site of the new town Cambourne. In the end, she tactfully arrived on 6 September 1967, which is my birthday – my best present ever.

Again I missed the birth and, in Cambridge, was woken with the news at 7.30 a.m. My job was to take Hal, aged two and a half, round to the family retainer Mrs Parker a couple of streets away. It was a superb early autumn morning and I put Hal in the bike basket with his legs hanging out and cycled through the empty streets to leave him there for the day.

Married a thatched cottage

Clare's mother had grown up in Letchworth, taken a job in North Hertfordshire, and bought Paddocks Wells in 1938. Its refrigerator was acquired during the Munich crisis. She and her husband Henry offered to give the cottage to their three children – Lyn, Chris and Clare. However, her brothers had young families and felt reluctant to take on the responsibility of looking after it. Clare could not bear to lose it. She teased me that I only married her for Paddocks Wells.

At the time, people did not talk about mortgages. In fact, when playing Monopoly I had no idea what a 'mortgage' was – possibly a disease! The problem was whether I could commute from Stevenage to Farringdon to work at Oxford University Press, which was between the Old Bailey and St Paul's. I would take the Circle line from Farringdon to St Paul's.

My South African grandmother, Edith Vinnicombe, had come to Britain at the end of the nineteenth century to attend the renowned Glasgow College of Art. She told me that the underground trains on the Circle line had been pulled by coal-fired locomotives and that the stations and tunnels were full of smoke.

Paddocks Wells in Cottered consisted of two classic Hertfordshire wood-framed and thatched houses centred on two massive red brick chimneys with inglenook fireplaces backing onto one another. They had for several centuries provided central heating by storing heat from continuously burning wood fires. The bread was baked on oven floors made intensely hot with ashes, which were raked out before the roundels of dough were slid in on paddles. A passageway joining the two parts of the cottage had been constructed by removing one of the ovens.

One Christmas, I was given a homebrew kit for making Newcastle Brown ale. When I failed to do so, Hal, aged about ten, thought it ought to be put to good use, but the bottles blew under fermentation and brown liquid oozed through the white ceiling.

With two growing children we decided we ought to build an extension, including a second bathroom, at the village end of the thatched cottage.

Since Clare and I had been very impressed by the design of the roofs at the Welwyn Garden City swimming baths, when it came

James Currey's Heinemann African department visit Paddocks Wells, Cottered. The extension is new.

to hiring Clare's parents' architect, Leonard Brown, to draw up our plans, we decided to ask him to incorporate their shape into his plans. Consequently, the garden-facing walls were made of glass from floor to ceiling to take advantage of the view of the greenery in the substantial garden.

We had always admired the skill of Mr Newman, the joiner and carpenter from the village, and the whole project was planned in wood to take advantage of his skills (as Clare and I were to do again in the kitchen at Walkern Mill). The public sides were made from grey fireproof lap boarding, which Tamsin's escaped pony started to kick one Sunday morning when Hal was in bed inside.

Horses

Adjoining Walkern Mill was a quarter-mile-long paddock in which the miller had grazed his carthorses. There were also two

Renovated Walkern Mill with its lucom where sacks of grain had been hoisted off wagons for milling. The Miller's Cottage is on the bend on the road.

substantial stables clad with corrugated iron, which we replaced with, now revealed as toxic, asbestos cement panels on the roof and traditional lapboards on the sides. It had been built with wooden beams from the derelict mill.

Apart from Tamsin's horse – the elegant Jig – we gave grazing rights to a solid cob called Boy, whose owners happened to be away at the time for six months in Australia. Given that Clare's niece, her brother Chris's daughter Helen Wilson was a qualified riding instructor, I took the opportunity to get her to give me lessons when she was working on converting the mill. Being able to see over hedges from the saddle doubled one's view when out riding in the gently hilly countryside.

On one occasion, when I was galloping across a field in the fog, I went right through a herd of deer. On another, Clare and I set off over a long field of stubble. I could hear her horse pounding behind me, but when I turned round Clare was no longer in the saddle. Horrified, I cantered back to find her lying on the stubble.

I gathered the reins of her horse and went to the road to stop a car. It was rapidly getting dark and I stood by the roadside with the two horses. A car came almost at once and I managed to stop it. It then started to accelerate away but stopped in response to my yells. Clare then staggered down the bank and the driver took her to the mill while I led the two horses home. I took her to A&E in Stevenage where they cleared her to come home.

Tamsin had a riding companion, the builder's daughter Sarah Mortar. As dusk was approaching one evening, and both families were anxiously scouring the landscape as it grew increasingly darker, to our relief we suddenly heard them singing in the hills.

Contributions to Cottered village

The A road past the cottage was filled with lorries, particularly from the new Sainsbury's depot in Buntingford. Soon after we settled in Cottered, Clare mounted a campaign to get the East Herts Council to build a tarmacked footpath along the verge.

Pushing Hal in his buggy and armed with a petition for the neighbours to sign, she visited every house in the village, so quickly got to meet the other villagers. Her breakthrough came when she got a letter about the footpath printed in *The Times*. Only then did the East Herts Council act.

In an obituary following Clare's death, Juliet Clough pointed out in 'Other Lives' in the *Guardian* (6 June 2016) that 'women were often at the centre of Clare's concerns, particularly women in education. When we were living in rural Hertfordshire, she encouraged women who might not otherwise have considered doing so to take A Levels at the local comprehensive school and even get to Cambridge.'

Rose Luce and Clare set up a playgroup in the old wartime hut bought from the searchlight detachment and rebuilt at the top of the garden alongside the wartime pigsty – a pig for victory! I dug a sandpit for the playgroup with Richard Luce, later to be Governor of Gibraltar and then Lord Chancellor at Windsor Castle.

ESCAPE FROM SOUTH AFRICA

In 1982, Lord Carrington resigned as foreign minister because he accepted that the Foreign Office had failed to warn of the danger of the Argentinians invading the Falkland Islands; it is often cited as the last time a minister resigned and Richard Luce resigned with him. When he had stood in Stevenage as the Conservative candidate against the renowned Labour politician Shirley Williams, Clare said, 'Richard, why on earth do you want to become a Conservative MP?' He replied, 'duty!' His father had been a governor of a province of Sudan.

Our neighbours on the corner later persuaded Clare to stand for the parish council to stop the one candidate, a former RAF officer, from being elected unopposed. Although Clare did not even turn up for the count in the village hall, there had been a tie, and Neville Chuck, a reporter on the *Royston Crow*, had to rush down the high street to fetch her so that the result could be decided through drawing lots – Clare emerged the winner. Although she was an assiduous councillor, she found it took a lot of her time and so she did not stand at the next election.

I volunteered to organise the annual village bonfire for Guy Fawkes and, for several years in October, would recruit the help of a farmer to go round the village with his tractor and trailer to collect the autumn brushwood. I was relieved to get the village policeman Mr Silsby to organise the fireworks display with appropriate discipline.

Both Hal and Tamsin went to the Cottered primary school, which Hertfordshire County Council had rebuilt in stylish modern architecture and which, as it was Anglican, the Bishop of St Alban's had opened.

Its head was keener on tidiness than on teaching and we thought that nobody would offer him a job because of the poor references we, the governors, gave him. Fortunately, a school in Norfolk, which neglected to take up his references, took him off our hands. We later heard that the Norfolk school had also found him uninspiring.

There is a photograph of six-year-old Hal lecturing his classmates on how Mr Pledger was rethatching the ridge of our cottage.

Clare wrote to me in Africa saying that the 'the young builder is busy in his sandpit.' When Hal was older he helped me build a multi-storeyed tree house in an elm (doomed to die from the tragic Dutch elm disease). Clare knew that I had strongly considered training as an architect, so was anxious about me pushing Hal too hard in that direction.

The first book published by Clare and James Currey

The first time I saw a Range Rover was when the new model, just bought by a parent, was used to pick up and take several Cottered children, including ours, to St Christopher School in Letchworth. The school was well-known as a vegetarian boarding school, which was unusual in the 1970s. Clare joined the parent's committee, but felt annoyed because it was so slow to produce ideas for fundraising. I said, 'what about editing and publishing a vegetarian cookbook?' After having put the idea to the committee, Clare came home furious because the committee had turned it down on the grounds that it was worried about paying the printer. I then suggested that she and I publish it together.

The parents would be sure to pay up front when they placed their orders and the printers would give us three months' credit. Clare then set out to collect recipes from the parents. The recipes from committed vegetarians tended to have puritanical names like 'Snelsmoor steamed savoury', so she discreetly went round her meat-eating friends to get some more interesting ones. Clare used an electric typewriter to produce the recipes in my interesting narrow format.

The demand for the *St Christopher Cornucopia* was immediate and we quickly had to reprint. When I visited the new Cranks restaurant-cum-bookshop in Soho, I was told that vegetarian cookbooks were few and far between and it took some copies into its stock. We later realised that this was the first publication made by Clare and me before we set up James Currey Publishers in 1985.

Women should be more adventurous

Clare always encouraged women to be more adventurous. Shirley Chesterman was continually being put down by her husband Jimmy, who had grown up in the shadow of his family's renowned Sheffield cutlery-making company and resented having missed out on a degree himself. Shirley had trained as a nurse and he used to belittle her, so when the Open University was being founded in 1969, Clare suggested to Shirley that they should do a degree together!' Disappointingly, Shirley dropped out, but Clare, although a young mother, kept going and much enjoyed studying and getting a second degree in art history, especially since she felt that her third-class Oxford degree was less of an achievement than it in fact was.

She then managed to persuade a friend who had left school at 16 to enrol for the sixth form at the new Ward Freeman comprehensive school in Buntingford in Hertfordshire to study for an A Level in English, which was to lead on to her getting a place at the new Lucy Cavendish College at Cambridge University.

Clare decided to join her at Ward Freeman, where Patrick Nobes was headmaster and Alistair Langford the English teacher. They became friends and then, to our surprise, were appointed as headmaster of Bedales and head of the junior school at Bedales at Petersfield in Hampshire respectively.

Bedales just right for Hal

We had put Hal's name down for Bedales, for we had always had that school in mind for him. It had potential pupils come to try boarding for two nights while they took their tests. Hal came back desperate to be chosen. It was to prove to be a success for him. Tamsin was a less conventional achiever and made herself ill on the two test boarding nights at Bedales. Patrick Nobes was embarrassed when he rang to tell us that she had not been accepted and he was surprised to hear she would hate to go. She chose a comprehensive school in Stevenage, which set her mathematics and sciences straight after easy-going St Christopher.

Sir John Newsom, the renowned director of education for Hertfordshire, had after the war taken advantage of the new towns of Stevenage, Welwyn Garden City, Letchworth and Hertford to pioneer comprehensive schools and lead the country towards abolishing the eleven-plus entry to grammar schools. (He came to speak to the Oxford International Committee conference at Oxford.)

Two years later we took Tamsin on a grand tour of progressive schools and she chose Abbotsholme, a mildly original school in Derbyshire described as a less demanding Bedales.

Quakers

Clare's parents, Henry and Ruth Wilson, were active in Meetings for Sufferings, which is what the Quaker executive committee is called. Several of Clare's family were involved in the Society of Friends. In fact, Clare herself was quite committed to the Quakers and chose to get married in the Friends Meeting House near her parents home in Cambridge.

To get married on 21 December 1962, we merely stood up in the Friends Meeting House and each gave our word to the other. I said to her 'I take thee my friend Catherine Clare Wilson to be my wife.' In like manner, Clare then took me to be her husband. Then all we had to do was to sign some papers afterwards. Then, after we had agreed to marry one another, the meeting for worship continued in silence during which my grandfather, the Methodist minister J. P. Martin, gave an inspired extempore prayer.

When the children were young, Clare took them to Quaker meetings in Stevenage. I would go to meetings with her for family occasions. I had a greater admiration for the Friends than for any other religious group.

Clare's mother Ruth said she wished she lived in a house big enough for all three of her families to stay together. Each Easter, she generously paid for everybody to stay at Glenthorne, a Quaker guesthouse in Grasmere in the Lake District, and we would go out walking on the fells every day. It was equipped with fine drying rooms and everybody joined in with the washing up.

Hal was old enough to stand up for himself against his older cousins and was fond of Eleanor. Tamsin was very much younger than her cousins and had to be protected from their bullying. Once I walked with her in the mist all the way up to Skafell Pike; she thought I had tricked her and was furious. Her female cousins refused to believe that she had gone there. Lyn was chief prefect and, on one walk when some visiting cousins were there, he said to me, 'let's burn them off!'

Tresco and the Isles of Scilly

Clare realised that the Isles of Scilly would be special, so when a visiting African author left behind a copy of the *Daily Telegraph* containing a small advertisement for a house with ten beds called Ocean View, we decided to rent it. The idea was to spend two or three days at the New Inn before moving across to Tresco, where Lyn and Jeanetta and their four children would be joining us at Ocean View, which looked out towards St Martin's.

In July/August 1972, Clare, Hal, Tamsin and I were on the beach below Cromwell's castle talking to a young German couple from Munich; they were staying at the New Inn to avoid the Olympic Games, which were being held in Munich that year. Suddenly, a boat came speeding up the sound and headed into our little bay. A man in a black wetsuit (possibly the first time I had seen a wetsuit) jumped out and strode towards us with outstretched hand saying, 'I'm Robin Hanbury-Tenison – explorer.' Where does an explorer go on holiday?

ESCAPE FROM SOUTH AFRICA

Tresco in the Isles of Scilly. This is the view down from King Edward's Castle, past Cromwell's Tower and over the channel to Bryer. Hal and Tamsin asked Clare, as she was dying, what was her favourite view. This was it!

They were staying at Bay House. His party, most of whom were to arrive on the Isle of Man lifeboat, was already unpopular with the Tresco estate management company. Some friends of theirs from Cornwall flew round Bay House dipping the wings of their planes.

They had had a far more exciting time in Cornwall, though, where they had crashed their Land Rover while trying out a drogue for hang gliding along the seashore. 'Only one person broke his leg!' Robin's first wife Marika Hanbury-Tenison's Cornish cookery books were to be among Clare's favourites.

A timeshare at Bay House

In 1980 we heard that Bay House would be offering time-shares on 40-year leases. Would we ever be able to go there again? We rationalised that if we bought a timeshare in a large house overlooking the sea for a fortnight during the July/August school holidays then we would sell on the time share every other year. We sold the fortnight only once.

It cost us a lot to get there, albeit on a wonderful journey – sleeper from Paddington to Penzance and then helicopter to the main island, St Mary's.

Swimming accident between Bryher and Tresco

Bay House looked out onto Bay Beach. Fortunately, the water between the islands is slightly warmer than the surrounding Atlantic. I went for long swims most days, often close to Bryher, the parallel island. One fine morning I went right over to Bryher and could have phoned the boat company to come and collect me. There were several yachts moored across the channel. There were two men active on one of the yachts.

I decided, even although I was cold, that it would be good to swim back to the Tresco quay via the three yachts. I was about half way across when suddenly a tidal surge came down the channel and I became nervous and shouted to the men on the yacht. They climbed into their outboard dingy and zipped over to me. Getting into a dingy from the water is always a struggle with your legs flailing around under the boat. They rushed me round to Bay House beach, but I was suffering from either hypothermia or an oedema caused by my struggle to get into the dingy.

They got poor Clare down from Bay House. A leading British heart specialists on holiday was walking past and he said calmly to Clare, 'he'll be all right.' They got me on a trolley up to the heliport and summoned a helicopter from Fleet Air Arm at Culdrose in Cornwall. About half way there a flying officer clambered over to Clare at the back and told her that I was taking an interest in the countryside.

At Truro Hospital they thought I might be suffering from blocked veins. I had to have a catheter slipped up into me and the male nurse told me that my veins were clear, which was not what everybody expected. Poor Clare had to fly back to Bay House after I had ruined our holiday.

When Clare was struggling with pain in her last days at the hospice, Hal and Tamsin asked her to think of her favourite views. She said they were down the New Grimsby Sound from King Charles, above Cromwell's castle and between Tresco and Bryher.

FOURTEEN
Thornhill Square, Caledonian Road

Up at Garnetts. 'Are these your Duncan Grants under mi paint pots?'

On our way south after an Easter stay in the Lake District, we called in to visit Ian and Lydia Wright in Manchester. Ian had been two years ahead of me at Kingswood and had then, at Oxford, got me involved in the Oxford International Committee. After a posting in the Far East, he became foreign editor of the *Manchester Guardian* in Manchester. Lydia told us that the foreign desk was moving to London and that they would be house-hunting.

Clare said we could do with a base in London and that perhaps by buying a terraced house together, we could have the basement as a flat for ourselves, with outside steps and shared access to a back garden. The Wrights needed room on the roof for their beehives. Lydia found 54 Thornhill Square just off the Caledonian Road and a mile up from King's Cross. Ian found a builder, Jack Bigsby, who spent most of the time converting their top four storeys but, when the Wrights were short of cash, would work on our basement flat.

Ian could usually stop Jack being taken away for urgent work for his other professional clients. Ian said: 'when Jack says he has to go and do work "up at Garnetts", you know what he means? He means Angelica Garnett of the Bloomsbury set who had lived with the artist Duncan Grant.' Once Hal and I were taking a lunch break in our basement, and Jack Bigsby was perched on a pile of flooring planks that were about to be laid. Jack Bigsby knew his Bloomsbury stories went down well with his patrons.

> O yes! The house was draped with cobwebs and she would wander around in her nightdress playing the violin in the candlelight. One time I was working in the kitchen and there was a knock on the front door. A gent said to me that he had come from the Tate Gallery to collect the paintings by Duncan Grant. I told him Mrs Garnett hadn't said nothing to me but he was welcome to look around. He came back into the kitchen and said he could not find them anywhere. I then asked him, 'are these them under mi paint pots?' He said, 'O yes! Stand back! Stand Back!'

A novel by Michael O'Hagan called *Caledonian Road* was published in 2024. The hero, Professor Campbell Flynn lives in Thornhill Square, a couple of doors down from where we and the Wrights were. People trafficking was the new subject.

Dragged down by Alzheimer's

On 9 May 2020 I rang Anthony Wilson in Lichfield. He had enjoyed my account in the *New African* of our visit to them in Nyasaland. He had especially liked the picture of the minister John Dunstan Msonthi on the ferry, whom I had quoted as saying that the Dr (by which he meant Banda), might sack him tomorrow. In fact, a fortnight later the Dr had staged a virtual coup and had indeed sacked half his cabinet.

Anthony had Anne with Alzheimer's beside him. He said that I must have had a tough time with Clare, but nothing compared with what he had been going through with Anne. With Clare, it was a sad decline into deafness – no longer laughing together; not hearing one another; forgetting to take my phone upstairs to the top floor so she could phone me when she needed me.

Mary Dyson and I become colleagues

As I mentioned earlier, in 1967 Oxford University Press moved to Ely House, which had formerly been the Albemarle Ladies Club, in the West End. It was a case of 'I dreamt I dwelt in marble halls.' I was given a desk across one corner of an enormous office at the top of the building and, directly opposite, was a new editor called Mary Dyson, a trainee just down from Cambridge. We went out to lunch together and became fellow publishers and lifelong friends.

Our boss Anthony Toyne was an Old India Hand with all the worst imperial aspects of that description – he looked down on colonials from Africa. Mary was to train to work with Tsefaye Daba who was opening an OUP office in Addis Ababa.

I had told David Neal and Philip Chester that I wanted, after having been in South Africa for five years, to spend some time from 1964 in the London office. However, in late 1966 I was pressed to take an OUP job in Nigeria.

Since Clare had already had a miscarriage and if, as we hoped, she were again to become pregnant, we would in no way want her to have to rely on the Nigerian maternity services. I therefore declined the offer. It was awkward, but Philip Chester was understanding. John Brown disapproved.

Headhunted by Heinemann

I was cheerfully comfortable at OUP, but kept an eye on the appointments section at the back of *The Bookseller*. For three weeks at the end of 1966, an advertisement was placed for an African job at Heinemann. Rex Collings said, 'are you putting in for that Heinemann job? It looks ideal for you.' I mentioned the ad to Clare when driving back from Hugo Brunner's wedding near Henley. We thought I might as well apply. I worked on my CV and on the

THORNHILL SQUARE, CALEDONIAN ROAD

Monday dropped in the submission at 48 Charles Street in Mayfair. By return, I was given an appointment with Alan Hill, the managing director.

The interview went quite slowly to begin with while we talked about textbooks. Then, almost shyly, Alan said, 'well, what do you think about our African Writers Series?' At that point, the interview took off. I could not believe Alan Hill's enthusiasm. Alan Hill's version was, 'I headhunted James Currey from Oxford University Press.'

At OUP, Rex Collings's Three Crowns series was doubtfully being kept going for public relations reasons to justify the enormous profits being made selling textbooks in the Third World.

Alan Hill told me that I would have an interview with Keith Sambrook after he got back from the Caribbean. The interview was at 6.00 p.m. and after ten or so minutes Keith Sambrook said 'Let's go round to the pub!' and we talked for three hours.

I had to work out my three-months' notice until the end of March 1967. Keith Sambrook got me round to meet Chinua Achebe on his way to America at the time when the Biafran crisis was turning into a civil war. I took a manuscript that I had failed to get Toyne to accept. It was a collection of stories by Tayeb Salih called *The Wedding of Zein*. Achebe and Sambrook immediately started turning over the pages and Chinua Achebe said after a few minutes 'This man can write!' They wanted to accept it.

At OUP they had wanted to reject it. In 2025 his novel *Season of Migration to the North* about seamy 1930s London in the land of 'jig-jig' had been in print for well over fifty years.

FIFTEEN
African Writers Series

'Penguin Books for Africa'

People often credit me with starting the African Writers Series but I came in when it was already well established with some 30 titles chosen by Alan Hill and Keith Sambrook. By the time I left, there were 270 titles; Vicky Unwin had added about a hundred. Almost certainly, I was made a fellow of the Royal Society of Literature in 2003 in recognition of my work towards the worldwide establishment of African literature.

In 1958, James Michie at William Heinemann had published about two thousand hardback copies of Chinua Achebe's *Things Fall Apart*. In 1959, the educational manager Alan Hill decided to visit Ghana, which had become independent in 1957, and Nigeria, which was due to become independent in 1960. In Nigeria, he expected to be praised for the publication of Chinua Achebe's novel, but nobody seemed to have seen it. They said, 'you mean a novel written by that young man down at federal broadcasting in Lagos?' In 1959, Alan Hill realised that a cheap paperback series, a 'Penguin Books for Africa', was needed as the decolonisation of the French and English colonies took off.

In July 1962, the Congress for Cultural Freedom in Paris funded a conference of 'African Writers of English Expression' at Makerere University in Uganda, and flew in writers and publishers. It turned out to be a major landmark in the establishment of African literature. It was revealed in 1967 that the Congress for Cultural Freedom was set up to disguise the fact that it was CIA funded, but we were deep into the cold war and Russia supported communist journals and distributed free books. John Hunt at the

Congress for Cultural Freedom in Paris made money available to support journals and books that spread the ideas of the 'Free World'. Randolph Vigne and Neville Rubin also got Congress to fund the radical monthly, the *New African*, which was an immediate success; Randolph said he thought my adventurous page design drew attention to the journal.

For the Makerere meeting in 1962, Alan Hill and Van Milne rushed out the first four titles in the African Writers Series – reprints of the first two Achebe novels, a Cyprian Ekwensi novel, and Kenneth Kaunda's *Zambia Shall Be Free*. They shamelessly used Penguin's orange, blue and brown colours for the covers and were amazed by the size of the immediate orders from booksellers, especially in Nigeria, Kenya and South Africa.

One morning at the Makerere conference in July 1962, Achebe opened his resthouse door to find a student called James Ngugi asking him to read two manuscripts called *The River Between* and *Weep Not, Child*. Achebe read them that night and at breakfast got Van Milne to ring Alan Hill in England to say he ought to accept sight unseen. Alan Hill, who had been summoned from a board meeting, agreed.

In December 1962 Alan Hill invited Chinua Achebe to be editorial adviser for the series because he would be a magnet for young writers. On 1 January 1963 Keith Sambrook joined Heinemann from Thomas Nelson and found the manuscripts of Ngugi's *Weep Not, Child* and *The River Between* on his desk.

SIXTEEN

The Establishment of African Literature

The breakthrough in the establishment of African literature

In July 1962, at the same time as the Makerere conference, the Congress for Cultural Freedom funded an equally important meeting at Fourah Bay College at the University of Sierra Leone. Representatives of university departments of English and education, still largely staffed by expatriates, made the historic decision to allow the West African Examination Council (WAEC) and the East African Examination Council (EAEC), to prescribe set books by contemporary African writers – albeit alongside Shakespeare and T. S. Eliot – because the students would feel a connection with them. The East African Council (EAEC) prescribed *Weep Not, Child* by Ngugi and, by the end of 1965, orders were coming in for 50,000 copies at a time.

Meanwhile, the francophone teachers attending a conference in Dakar decided on the opposite course and ruled that contemporary African writing should be confined to departments of anthropology and African studies. The East African board prescribed Mongo Beti's *Mission terminée*, translated as *Mission to Kala*, for the English exam, yet no French language board followed suit.

By 1 April 1967, which was when I joined Keith Sambrook, Aig Higo and he had got about thirty-five titles into print in the African Writers Series and unsolicited manuscripts were arriving by every post from Africa. Undoubtedly, the excitement of seeing the photographs of black faces on the back made young Africans feel they might have a chance of getting published in London. Chinua Achebe said it was as though lock gates had been opened and that he was flooded by manuscripts 'good, bad and indifferent'.

Apparently, my predecessor at Heinemann had been overwhelmed and Alan Hill and Keith Sambrook found that she was literally sitting on unopened parcels under the cushion on her chair. One morning I sat on the other side of Keith Sambrook's desk and we team-read the revised manuscript of Ayi Kwei Armah's *The Beautyful Ones Are Not Yet Born*. Aig Higo and Keith Sambrook had already sent first reports to Ayi Kwei Armah.

'I tell you Chief Fagunwa was murdered!'

The first manager in Ibadan in Nigeria was Chief Fagunwa, who drowned in a ferry accident on the River Wuya in Bida. At a party at the Hotel Bristol in Lagos, the voice of the novelist Cyprian Ekwensi rose above the hubbub: 'I tell you, Chief Fagunwa was murdered!' Keith Sambrook and Alan Hill then hired Aig Higo, a young school principal in the Mid-Western Region, and this had got Heinemann Nigeria off to a successful start by the time the tragic Biafran war had started in 1967.

In early 1968, I was sent off on my first West African tour of schools and universities in Sierra Leone, Ghana and Nigeria. Aig Higo in Ibadan, who was about ten years older than me, was very demanding and made it quite clear what he wanted.

On long car journeys he taught me the realities of publishing in Nigeria. Thanks to his contacts and close work with Chinua Achebe, the editor of the African Writers Series, they made an impressive start with the Nigerian and Ghanaian titles.

During the war, Chinua Achebe had managed to keep in touch with me in London when flying from the Uli Airstrip in Biafra via Lisbon to London. He was travelling on behalf of the Biafran foreign service, and I would keep a pile of reports on potential titles for the African Writers Series, which were ready to discuss

THE ESTABLISHMENT OF AFRICAN LITERATURE

(From left to right) Cyprian Ekwensi, Keith Sambrook, Alan Hill and James Currey (Nairobi 1974).

with him on the phone whenever he changed planes at Heathrow, which he frequently did.

In 1971, after the war had ended, for the first time I was allowed to travel to the predominantly Igbo area in the eastern part of Nigeria and to visit the University of Nigeria at Nsukka, which had been at the very centre of the Biafran intellectual resistance. The death in action during the war in 1967 of the poet, teacher, librarian, lover and gunrunner, Christopher Okigbo, sent shockwaves across Africa.

When I visited Chinua Achebe and his wife Christie at the University of Nsukka in 1971, the walls of their house were black and there was no electricity. The war had clearly taken its toll on Chinua Achebe, for during that time, he claimed that he had found it impossible to write anything more ambitious than poetry and short stories.

At his house in 1971 he gave me the manuscript of *Girls At War*, which was to become the one hundredth title in the series. In 1972, Alan Hill arranged that the publicity party for the first one hundred titles in ten years would be at the Athenaeum, the most renowned men's club in London.

THE ESTABLISHMENT OF AFRICAN LITERATURE

Henry Chakava, editor in Nairobi, in my office in London, 1973.

At his house at Nsukka he had said that he ought to hand over the editorship of the African Writers Series and we had agreed that Ngugi, who was by now starting to use his original name of Ngũgĩ wa Thiong'o, would be the obvious choice. Ngugi accepted the offer, but then understandably said that the job would interfere with his own writing. So, in 1972, it was agreed that Henry Chakava in Nairobi, Aig Higo and Akin Thomas in Ibadan, and I in London would form an editorial triangle. We got reports and circulated the shortlisted photocopies of manuscripts between all three offices.

When Ngugi was released from detention in 1980, the University of Nairobi disgracefully refused to reappoint him as professor of English. Henry Chakava gave him a desk in his Heinemann office so that he had a base in central Nairobi.

Ngugi wanted to show me his new house, which he boasted

THE ESTABLISHMENT OF AFRICAN LITERATURE

(From left to right) James Currey and Aig Higo from Nigeria with Bob Markham at his office in Nairobi.

his royalties from Heinemann had paid for. He had got the School of Architecture to draw on traditional features in a modern house, but designed around a cluster of seven huts. We sat in a circle in one of the rooms and a drinking horn was passed round the room from lip to lip. When Henry was driving me back to Nairobi I remarked on how interesting I had found the occasion. Henry said 'that's what I have to put up with when I go back to Kamusinga at Christmas.'

'In Nairobi even the streets are airconditioned'

When Aig Higo from Heinemann Nigeria first visited Nairobi he said that 'even the streets are airconditioned here!' Nairobi was booming and Bob Markham, a former librarian, ran its office. His wife was the redoubtable Susannah who, as a Jew, had fled from

Germany in the 1930s. Markham had been a flying boat pilot during the war and had landed many times on the Zambezi River between Northern and Southern Rhodesia.

In 1981, to publicise our new office in Zambia, he set up a book launch in Lusaka codenamed 'full bar with toasties' for when President Kenneth Kaunda, author of *Zambia Shall be Free*, launched the first Zambian novel. It was by Dominic Mulaisho and number 204 in the series. Dominic Mulaisho was managing director of the government-owned company MINDECO, which had nationalised 51 per cent of the minerals. Zambia was one of three great centres of copper mining. Dominic said to me, 'if I owned what I control, I would be the richest man in the world.'

In Ethiopia for the first week of the revolution against Emperor Haile Selassie

I used to feel lonely on these trips, which were essential to the growth of my African list, so managed to persuade Alan Hill to let Clare come with me on a visit to Kenya, Tanzania and Ethiopia in February 1974. We arrived on what turned out to be day two of the revolution that was to lead to Emperor Haile Selassie's overthrow. On day three of the revolution, our history author Merid Wolde Aregay took us into the market area. As we were being carried along by the excited crowd, he was saying, 'the emperor will appear.' When we reached the white Italian-built market building, the emperor appeared at the top of a sweep of steps and I vividly remember seeing him cast bank notes into the crowd. Clare, however, said that she had not seen the casting of the birr notes, and that I must have just read later accounts of it. By the end of that year the emperor had been deposed, taken off to prison in a Volkswagen Beetle and strangled.

At dawn on the Sunday we were taken high up above Addis Ababa to the round church of Entoto Mariam, where bare-footed peasant men in white clothes stood in the outer circle of the church,

THE ESTABLISHMENT OF AFRICAN LITERATURE

We visited the red monolithic churches below ground at Lalibela. It was the fifth day of the Ethiopian revolution.

as they had done for centuries before in this ancient Christian country.

There were disturbances over the weekend. On the Monday morning, the bookseller and author Daniachew Worku lent me his massive American car, but not before flipping open the glove compartment to show me his revolver. We stuck to our plans and flew north to Lalibela in Ethiopia with its monolithic red rock churches. The roofs of the buildings are at ground level so you have to go down steps to reach the floor.

Clare's parents and our helper Margery were looking after Hal and Tamsin and, on John Craven's News Round, had been watching daily reports of the revolution in the country in which their parents were travelling. It was day eight of the revolution when calm and efficient Ethiopian Airlines flew us back to London. The window of the airline bus was broken and, later that day, the Addis Ababa airport was closed and remained so for weeks. Unfortunately, we had arrived in London a little too late to vote in the British general election – we had gone from revolution to democracy in one day.

We published two editions of Bahru Zewde's *A History of Modern Ethiopia*. Donald Crummey said, 'the account of the revolution, contained in 41 pages, is nuanced and worthy of attention in its own right.'

Banned from Nigeria for having worked in South Africa

Of course, it would have been valuable to go on publishing visits to South Africa, but I had received a letter from South Africa House saying that I would need to apply for permission to go there. Perversely, I was also failing to get clearance for a visitor's permit for my next visit to Nigeria. Aig Higo found out from a university friend in the Lagos foreign ministry that it was because I had worked in South Africa. I was given no credit for having helped a South African activist escape.

Aig accompanied me to the Nigerian passport office behind a shop front in Fleet Street. Without bothering to report to reception, he burst straight into an office where piles of passports were heaped up against the walls. The clerk found mine lying in a corner among those of many other visa applicants. Aig then thrust it before the official and, there and then, got him to 'chop' it, namely to give it the relevant stamp.

The first Nobel Prize for an African writer

In the early 1980s, Rex Collings used to get his friends to gather each year in the Africa Centre to wait to see if that year Wole Soyinka would at last win the Nobel Prize in Literature. Rex had published Soyinka's work at both OUP and Methuen, so when he set up Rex Collings Ltd, Soyinka went with him. (After his trips to Africa or America, Soyinka would use the whole floor of Rex's office to sort out his post.)

THE ESTABLISHMENT OF AFRICAN LITERATURE

In 1986, with wide open arms Rex Collings walked onto the Africa Centre's decorative Victorian cast-iron orange balcony to announce that Wole Soyinka had won the Nobel Prize in Literature – the first black African writer ever to do so.

Long days of travel in Africa by car or plane were always memorable for the opportunity they provided for long talks. On a plane back from a conference in Zanzibar, I once had an enjoyable talk with Abdulrazak Gurnah, who in 2021 was also awarded the Nobel Prize in Literature. In March 2025, it was good to hear him being interviewed on Radio 4 and giving a talk in the Sheldonian.

Two other Nobel Prize winners were pleased to be included in the African Writers Series. Qualification for inclusion in the series was that writers had to have either been 'born in Africa or to have passed their formative years there'. That was to accommodate Doris Lessing's *The Grass is Singing* since she had been born in Persia.

I asked Nadine Gordimer which novel or short story collection she would like to represent her in the African Writers Series. She suggested assembling a group of her stories set in Africa and then to send those to my colleagues in Nairobi and Ibadan for consideration. We quietly agreed that if they were not keen then we would drop the proposal. They came back with substantial orders. Nadine Gordimer expressed great admiration for the presentation of our edition, but saw her Penguin editions as disastrous.

SEVENTEEN
Key African Writers

I added 250 titles to the Heinemann African Writers Series. They were numbered on the spine from 1 to 270. There were 400 titles by 2003 when new management under new owners closed the series down. In London, famous paperback publishers like Penguin and Pan subcontracted their books from established hardback publishers. Later, we could follow that tradition with the Caribbean Writers Series because several London publishers, such as André Deutsch, had regularly published new Caribbean writers during the 1950s.

Keith Sambrook rapidly ran out of published African titles to put in the African Writers Series and so decided to publish new novels in both hardback and paperback. This was a major initiative and some authors stand out. From among the 400 titles in the African Writers Series, I have selected some of the most successful ones to give an idea of how we all worked together.

Chinua Achebe

Professor Simon Gikandi of Princeton said that 'Achebe is the man who invented African literature because he was able to show, in the language and structure of *Things Fall Apart*, that the future of African writing did not lie in simple imitation of European forms but in the fusion of such forms with the oral traditions.'

There could not have been a more appropriate novel with which to start the African Writers Series than *Things Fall Apart*. Its central character is a wrestler called Okonkwo whose fate is echoed

KEY AFRICAN WRITERS

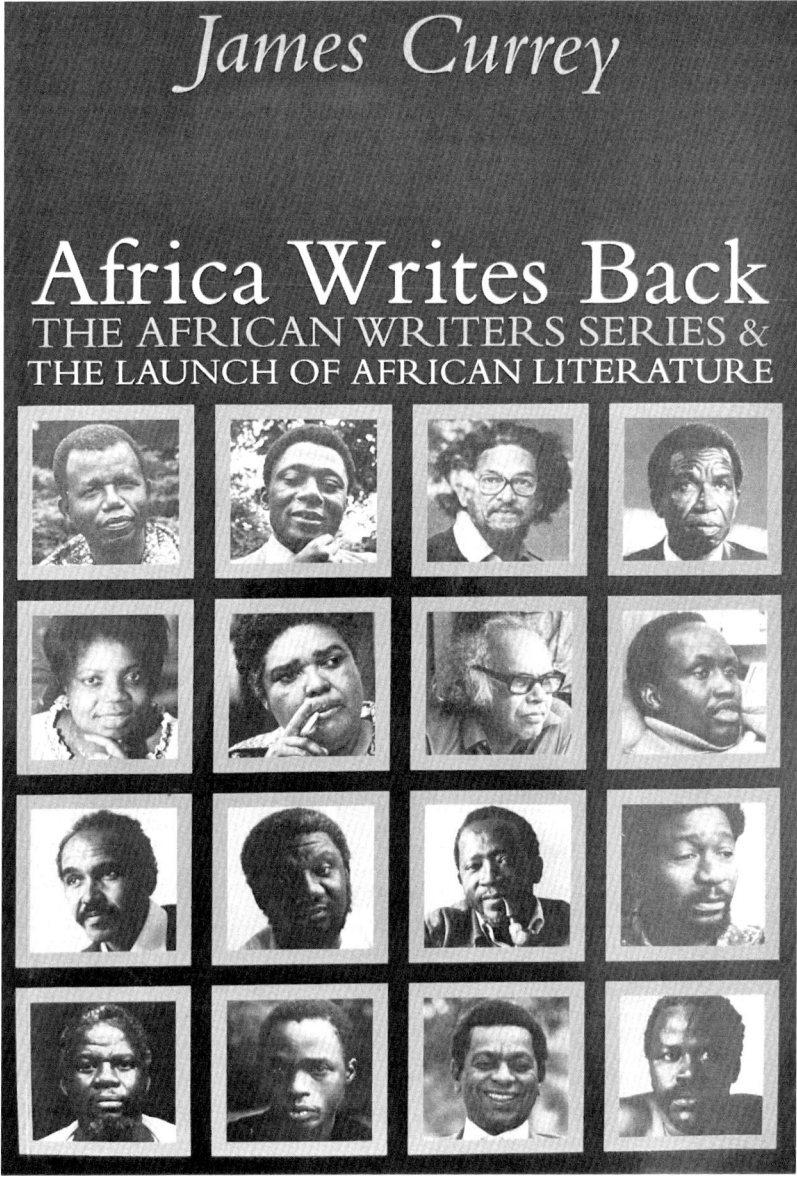

Top row: *Chinua Achebe, Mongo Beti, Dennis Brutus, Cyprian Ekwensi*
2nd row: *Buchi Emecheta, Bessie Head, Alex la Guma, Ngugi wa Thiong'o*
3rd row: *Nuruddin Farah, Ousmane Sembène, F. Oyono, Wole Soyinka*
Bottom row: *Mazisi Kunene, Marechera, Tayeb Salih, and Taban lo Liyong.*

in the collapse of the African way of life. It was published at the same time as Achebe's third title in the series, called *No Longer at Ease*. Two more of Achebe's novels – *Arrow of God* and *A Man of the People*, the latter of which prophesied the Biafran war – were to follow and were numbers 16 and 31 in the African Writers Series respectively. Then, *Anthills of the Savannah* was published in 1987.

The sales in English of *Things Fall Apart* were estimated to have passed the ten million mark by the turn of the century, although his publishers have by now totally lost count. Translations have appeared in most of the published languages.

As the founding editor of the African Writers Series, Achebe made a creative contribution to the establishment of African writing as a world literature, and his supporters feel that he should have been awarded the Nobel Prize.

Elechi Amadi

Captain Elechi Amadi of the Nigerian Military School in Zaria, with the meticulous organisational skills of a soldier, completed the carefully constructed trilogy of *The Concubine* (no. 25 in the series), *The Great Ponds* (no. 44) and *The Slave* (no. 210) between 1966 and 1978. An East African reader was disappointed that, after 200 titles in the African Writers Series, he was taking us back to the period in which Achebe's *Things Fall Apart* had been set.

The African Writers Series' paperback editions only reached Nigeria in 1966, which was not that long before the beginning of the Biafran War. In 1968, Aig Higo reported that 'Elechi lost his job and was detained by [President] Ojukwu in July 1967. He only escaped when Federal Forces liberated Port Harcourt. Between July 1967 and 1968, he had not received any salary, so he was really desperate when he came into my office.'

The war deeply affected Amadi's personal and writing life and he was, with his military background, to write one of the very best accounts of the war called *Sunset in Biafra* (African Writers Series no. 140). His fourth novel – *Estrangement* (African Writers Series no. 250) – proved to have all too appropriate a title because by then I had left Heinemann to set up my own business. He wrote to my successor saying that 'James Currey was a personal friend and his departure makes me sad.' The manuscript arrived just around the time when the Nigerian foreign exchanges closed in April 1982, after which it took years of negotiation to secure the foreign currency needed to meet a percentage of the debts incurred during the years of the oil boom when *The Concubine* and other books were flooding into Nigeria. By 1982, sales of *The Concubine* had approached 300,000.

Ngugi wa Thiongo'o

Ngugi's novels *Weep Not, Child* (no. 7) and *The River Between* (no. 17) became instantly known because the new postcolonial exam boards in East and West Africa had decided to prescribe new books by African writers alongside those of writers such as Shakespeare and Wordsworth. On 1 January 1963, when Keith started at Heinemann, he found on his desk the manuscript of *Weep Not, Child*. The immediate success of the Ngugi and Achebe novels encouraged Heinemann to put new work by unpublished authors into the African Writers Series. However, Ngugi was first and foremost a playwright, and his plays such as *Ngaahika Ndenda* were more effective in Gikuyu.

His message was that the British had made their decolonisation deal with the loyalists and that ordinary peasants, from whom the freedom fighters had been drawn, had been robbed. This was not what the Kenyan elite wanted to hear. In *Detained* (no. 240, p. xvi), Ngugi writes that 'some time in December, two gentlemen, highly placed in the government, flew to Mombasa and demanded an urgent audience with Jomo Kenyatta. They each held a copy of *Petals of Blood* in one hand, and in the other a copy of *Ngaahika Ndenda*.' On the last day of that year Ngugi was detained in Kamiti Maximum Security Prison in Nairobi and, at the end of 1978, he emerged from prison brandishing the manuscript of *Devil on the Cross* (African Writers Series no. 200) written on toilet paper. This 'same old decent toilet paper which has been useful to Kwame Nkrumah in James Fort Prison, Dennis Brutus on Robben Island, Abdilatif Abdalla in G Block in Kamiti and countless other persons with simple urges – has enabled me to defy the detention of my mind' (*Detained*, p. 6).

Alex La Guma

When I joined Heinemann I had no idea that so many of our authors would be detained because of their published work. Alex La Guma's novel, *A Walk in the Night*, was set in District Six, which supplied labour for the Cape Town docks. It was said that one reason why Christiaan Barnard was able to carry out the world's first heart transplant was because, after a weekend in District Six, there were so many stabbings that the surgeons at the nearby Groote Schuur Hospital had more practise in heart surgery than they would ever get at any other hospital. La Guma's *The Stone Country* was set in Roeland Street Prison, which you pass every time you leave the motorway into Cape Town from the comfortable southern suburbs. Robben Island prison is visible across the glittering waters of Table Bay.

Dennis Brutus

Dennis Brutus's poems, *Letters to Martha*, were written on postcards as continuous prose and sent from the island to his sister-in-law. When Brutus was being driven into Johannesburg after the South African Special Branch had arrested him on the border of Swaziland, he feared that nobody would know he had been brought back into the republic and that the Special Branch might well murder him. He jumped out of the car and was shot in the back outside the Rand Club where millionaire mine owners were having their lunch. After a spell in hospital, he was sent to Robben Island. His crime was that he had started the South African Non-Racial Olympic Committee (SAN-ROC), which succeeded in getting the white South African rugby team excluded from taking part in the Olympic Games by persuading the New Zealand All Blacks not to play against an all-white South Africa. The South African government considered him to be one of its ten most dangerous men.

Nuruddin Farah

Nuruddin Farah was one of the most outstanding of the unpublished writers I discovered. One Sunday evening I was so gripped by his *From a Crooked Rib* (African Writers Series 80) that I took the manuscript to bed with me in an attempt to finish reading it before morning. I remember how thoroughly annoying Clare found the sound of me turning the pages. Nuruddin Farah was forever amused that, in my acceptance letter after he had submitted the manuscript in 1968, I asked whether the writer was a man or woman. The writer had certainly portrayed the heroine Ebla with a female sensitivity. After taking a second husband to escape an arranged marriage, she argued that she was following the custom of men in a Muslim society who could choose to have more than one wife.

Dambudzo Marechera

My children called him 'Damn Boozo' and, by and large, he was exceedingly eccentric. When he first brought me the manuscript of *The House of Hunger* he boasted that he had tried to burn down New College, Oxford. Clare knew when I rang to tell her what train I was about to catch whether I had had a difficult day with him. He would repeatedly drag me into his theatre. In fact, he was dangerous.

I knew that he had pulled a knife on an architect who had taken him home to see his photographs of historic West African buildings. I was afraid he might attack my colleagues, or indeed me, and I was forever having to get him off the Heinemann premises.

On one occasion, he started to wrestle with me on the pavement of the square outside the three Heinemann houses, with people watching from the windows. He used to turn up at the reception in various disguises he had stolen by walking out dressed in them from theatrical outfitters. Once, when he was wearing a woman's dress, he asked for an advance of £50 so that he could go to Oxford. I said why didn't he hitchhike and he replied, 'what! Dressed like this?'

One sunlit morning a policeman rang to say that 'Mister Marrycheera' had been arrested for being drunk and disorderly and when taken into custody had 'thrown a punch at the super'. Would I stand surety for him at Clerkenwell courts? Again, I had to drop all my work for my other authors. The policeman at the court was reluctant to let me see him, so I pointed out that, if I were to stand surety, I needed to get the prisoner's assurance that he would turn up at court.

Reluctantly, he took me to the cell. Dambudzo Marechera was rattling away at the bars demanding that I get him out. When I could get him to listen, I said I was not going to risk my personal money if he was not going to attend court. 'Oh yes, of course I will! Get me out of here!' Rattle! Rattle! After a tense wait with my adrenalin flowing I was up before the beak myself. The magistrate asked me whether I could get the accused to court. I said I would do my best. 'What will happen if you fail?'

I took my long black Midland Bank cheque book out of my pocket, slapped it down and said, 'I suppose I will have to pay.' The magistrate barked, 'you are not a fit person to stand surety.' I said 'thank you' and left the dock a free man. A producer from the African Service also had his surety refused, so I did not feel too guilty about Dambudzo Marechera spending a week in prison before his case came up.

In 1979, when he won the Guardian Fiction Prize, at the prize ceremony in the Theatre Royal he started tossing plates at the vast wall mirrors. When Dagmar Heusler invited him to the Berlin Festival, he arrived at Heathrow with no passport or visitor's permit and walked out of Britain. Understandably, he was detained by the German frontier police. Dagmar Heusler got him out as she said he was performing the first evening, which he did with such great effect that he hit the headlines in the next day's German newspapers.

Bessie Head

Another writer of exceptional talent was the South African Bessie Head. She had had two novels published by Gollancz and Scribners, but they had rejected her autobiographical novel *A Question of Power (*African Writers Series no. 149*)*, which gave a horrifying insight into schizophrenia.

The African Writers Series was riding high in its tenth year and I got enthusiastic reports about her novel and acceptances from both Kenya and Nigeria within six weeks. Everybody felt it needed more work, but she was sensitive about criticism and had sacked her famous agent Hilary Rubenstein. I told him I would step forward into her firing line, but my acceptance had already given her the energy to revise. It was given a superb review by Ronald Blythe in *The Sunday Times* and it would eventually be taken over by Penguin Classics.

Women in Serowe in Botswana told their stories to Bessie Head with Chaucerian vividness and she put together a collection of them under the title *Botswana Village Tales*, which gave little warning of their ferocity. In the title story, *The Collector of Treasures*, the husband lies naked on their bed after returning from his concubine and his wife cuts off his genitals. When the police Land Rover delivers her to the prison, the women warder, 'with a flicker of humour', puts her in a cell with four other women who have killed their husbands.

David Philip accepted it for a South African edition. Bessie was delighted. 'Only you and I know the *anguish* of my life and I would have dreaded an adverse decision from him. As it is, I say, yippee.' There were postal hitches over the return of her manuscript for final work. There had been sabotage bombs on the railway line through Botswana and she wrote in October 1976: 'I had reduced the postal staff to the point of breakdown at the sight of me; six of them were on duty to instantly report the appearance of the typescript to me.'

I was worried about whether *Serowe: Village of the Rain Wind* (African Writers Series no. 220) would sell in the African Writers Series. Bessie Head makes people aware of their roots in Africa and, although she uses Serowe in Botswana, I hoped that people anywhere in Africa would make comparisons with experiences in their own societies. She explains that Serowe is a traditional African village in the sense that it is not a place of employment but a place of rest. The work areas are on the lands where they plough their crops and rear their cattle. She explains how Khama the Great opened up the whole society to make it receptive to new ideas, and how Tshekedi Khama laid the foundations for the type of free and experimental education that Patrick van Rensburg could build on.

Elspeth Huxley said in a review in *New Society* on 6 July 1981, 'Ronald Blythe's *Akenfield* has become a classic in the literature of English social history. I should be surprised if Bessie Head's *Serowe* did not win a similar place in the literature of post-independence Africa.' Bessie Head said: that,

> One of my problems is going to be how am I going to able to live in peace in Serowe once the book is published. There isn't a person in this village who will now not want the book. … I owe my 94 contributors a free copy each. But the story will never stop there. I know this village. The fence of this yard will be broken down by the people.

She was only due the six author copies written into her contract, but I managed to get her the 94 copies she needed for her neighbours.

Mazisi Kunene

Mazisi Kunene sent us three vast ill-organised manuscripts in Zulu verse. He managed to get a subsidy from the UNESCO translations scheme for *Emperor Shaka the Great* (African Writers Series no. 211). It made me face up to all sorts of questions about what we were trying to do in the African Writers Series, which was centred on the un-African concept of the novel. There was the question of authenticity. How did a publisher make the link to an audience reading the work of an oral tradition through the medium of English? Fortunately, my colleagues in the African companies thought that the work needed shaping with more of the mechanics of publishing, such as sections, introductions and notes.

After all our struggles Mazisi saluted the arrival of the first copy in 1979. 'Wonderful work. Congratulations on this masterly done book. I am certain the hero himself will be pleased.' Doris Lessing wrote to me, 'I am reading with total fascination, *Shaka*.' Most importantly, it was first published in Zulu. In 2005, Mazisi was made the first National Poet Laureate of South Africa.

Ayi Kwei Armah

The Ghanaian novel of corruption, *The Beautyful Ones are Not Yet Born* (African Writers Series no. 43), is as good as any other African novel. Here was a writer of astonishing self-assurance. The image of shit is embedded throughout the book. There is a description of a handrail encrusted with it from unwashed hands. At the time of a coup, the politician Abraham Koomson escapes through the night-soil hole out into the lane at the back of the house. He runs to the sea to plunge in his stinking clothes into a ritual cleansing. The trouble was that we were an educational publisher for African schools. Would we be able to sell a reasonable number?

Chinua Achebe shared Keith Sambrook's and my belief that we should accept all manuscripts of excellence regardless of sex, religion or politics. I used the surplus from the big-selling titles to risk a few titles like this, which would probably have low sales because its subject makes it difficult to use in schools. Our managing director Tony Beal sighed as he agreed that we had to do it. As hoped, sales quite quickly reached an initial 50,000.

Mongo Beti

Mission to Kala (African Writers Series no. 13) – a direct translation of *Mission terminée*) into English – was the first francophone novel to be included in the African Writers Series. The EAEC prescribed it in its African Writers Series English translation. When the copies arrived, the schoolteachers were upset, not so much by its gentle adolescent sex scenes as by its criticism of the Church. In Kenya, a delegation of women sought an audience with the minister of education's wife to protest about this set book, which they felt was an affront to African womanhood.

Mongo Beti, a Cameroonian, suspected correctly that his French publisher was not passing on his share of the English royalties. He contacted me directly. I listed the exact numbers of the ten English impressions of *Mission to Kala* between 1964 and 1974, which totalled 80,000 copies. Mongo Beti, very pleased, wrote to me saying that he had also looked through the sales figures with astonishment –'*J'ai aussi parcouru avec étonnement les chiffres de vente.*' Authors accept most things from their publishers, but if they start querying their royalties, then publishers must go out of their way to answer their worries in detail.

Cyprian Ekwensi

Cyprian Ekwensi's writing gave us the chance to see whether we could sell the African Writers Series in the general market both in Europe and Africa. The African market in English at the time of the Biafran War was educational. The general market was confined to the new campus bookshops in Africa and Europe. Heinemann's major market was based on educational institutions.

Cyprian Ekwensi wrote in 1976 that 'you already know my views on the snobbery with which Heinemann treats me and my work.' He was right. We considered him as a writer for the popular market and admired his professional story telling. Paul Richardson, who was the sales director, and I were especially keen to build up the bookshop sales for the African Writers Series in British bookshops.

Hutchinson had published *Jagua Nana* in 1961. Jagua is a prostitute who finances a teacher through law school in England on condition he marries her on his return to Nigeria. Heinemann did not publish it in the African Writers Series until 1975 (African Writers Series no. 146), by which time I could manage to get novels accepted that were unlikely to sell in schools.

Ekwensi survived the war as a chemist using his training in Chelsea. I had high hopes for his next novel about the aftermath of the Biafran War, *Survive the Peace* (African Writers Series no. 185). To my disappointment, Moira Lynd at William Heinemann did not recommend it for a hardback edition, so Heinemann Educational Books published it in hardback and paperback. He was complaining about the time we were taking to get through the press. I told him:

> We have to make sure that we have enough time to build up the publicity. Only yesterday I was having lunch with the literary editor of *The Sunday Times*, which is just about the most prestigious reviewing vehicle in London, and telling him about your novel. We are proud to be publishing it. We intend to give it the treatment it deserves.

Buchi Emecheta

Her four autobiographical novels were published in the Collins Fontana series for the British market. In 1979, she approached us with *The Joys of Motherhood* (African Writers Series no. 227) because she knew that the African Writers Series would get her into Africa. In 1994, when it was difficult to sell books to Africa, Heinemann bought the rights for six of her previously published titles set in England. She lived in England and the books went down particularly well in British schools where she became a popular speaker. They also appealed to the American market.

Ali A. Mazrui

Ali Mazrui was in 1965 made the first African professor of political science at Makerere. In 2005 the American journal *Foreign Affairs* selected him among 'the world's 100 leading intellectuals'.

I have published several of his books, including his one on the BBC Reith Lectures called *The African Condition*, and volume 8 of the UNESCO *General History of Africa*. He even published a political novel called *The Trial of Christopher Okigbo* (African Writers Series no. 97). 'The book uses as a central focus an imaginary courtroom in the hereafter at which Okigbo is charged with the sin of putting his tribe before his art as a poet. Behind it all is the Nigerian Civil War as a symbol of a continent in torment.' He said 'mine is a novel of ideas – violence, sex and poetry. A lot of Okigbo's poetry is woven into the narrative.'

Meja Mwangi

Henry Chakava got off to a good start in 1973 with the capture from the East African Publishing House (EAPH) of Meja Mwangi's *Kill Me Quick* (African Writers Series no. 143). As Ros de Lanerolle put it, it was 'really quite a find!' She described it is a:

> third-person autobiography (written as a novel but hero named Meja Mwangi) of a village boy who comes to Nairobi with a secondary certificate to get a job only to find

that, like thousands of others, he is unwanted. Makes friends with another boy in the same position, living off the rubbish in the backstreets. Both try to seek help from their families. They end up among the gangsters from the shanty towns, where they find comradeship but no escape from despair. Meja becomes a habitual criminal, his only home is jail.

Going Down River Road (African Writers Series no. 176) in 1976 led Michael Echeruo to reflect that Kenyan authors were writing about the town life of Kenya in a way that was little done in West Africa.

Naguib Mahfouz

Naguib Mahfouz was the best known author in the Arab world and *The Cairo Trilogy* is considered to be his greatest work. *Midaq Alley* (African Writers Series no. 151) is a novel of interlocking stories of people living in a Cairo street. It follows the life of a family through three generations from 1917 to 1944. Naguib Mahfouz called it 'a sequence of my country and myself'. The *Trilogy* was completed in 1952, the year of the revolt of young officers against Nasser, and there is a complex subtext in the book revealing the authoritarian regime. *The Sunday Times* gave it the headline of 'Earthier than Coronation Street'.

Mahfouz was awarded the Nobel Prize in Literature and survived an assassination attempt in 1994. This reinforced his popularity among Egyptians who felt that he was the embodiment of all that is best in their country – a champion of the poor, of women and the oppressed, an advocate of tolerance and social harmony. The religious authorities in Egypt had banned *Children of Gebelawi* by Naguib Mahfouz (now no. 15 in Heinemann's Arab Authors Series) and it was unbanned by none other than President Nasser himself. It was controversial because Mahfouz had described Gebelawi 'as an idea of God'.

The translator of his book, Philip Stewart, an Oxford academic studying for a doctorate in forestry in Cairo, had daily pasted the cuttings from its serialisation in *Al-Ahram* newspaper into a scrapbook, which he would deliver to Naguib Mahfouz every day while he was having his coffee in the cafe by the Cairo Opera House. Mahfouz had told this long, lanky Scot that he had no copy of his full-length book himself because the Beirut edition had been censored.

Philip Stewart's daughter lived near me in Oxford and, on his way to visit her he would, with delight, tell me about the latest development in the Mahfouz saga. *Miramar* (Arab Authors Series no. 9 and African Writers Series no. 197) was set in a hotel in Alexandria and had an introduction by John Fowles.

Denys Johnson-Davies had chosen not to translate Naguib Mahfouz because he was critical of his popular style characterised by what he considered sloppy repetition. I had a whole shelf of different translations made by Arabic speakers into English, which had been commissioned by the American University in Cairo Press; they were impossible to publish because they neglected the basic rule of literary translation, namely that translators should translate into their own languages. In 1988, Naguib Mahfouz became the first writer in Arabic to be awarded the Nobel Prize in Literature. As a result, he was stabbed in the throat by a religious fanatic, but fortunately survived the attack.

Tayeb Salih

Having failed to get Oxford University Press to accept *The Wedding of Zein* (African Writers Series no. 47), at our first meeting in February 1967 I tentatively showed this collection of Sudanese stories, which Denys Johnson-Davies had translated, to Chinua Achebe and he really liked it. It had remarkable illustrations by the Sudanese artist Ibrahim Salahi who had trained in Khartoum and at the Slade School of Fine Art in London.

One of my most remarkable days in Africa was when Ibrahim Salahi took me along the plots along the Nile near Khartoum, where peasant farmers were taking water out of the river with wooden machines invented several thousand years earlier. This was the very Nile that is almost a character in its own right in Tayeb Salih's writing. Denys Johnson-Davies worked with him on the English version of what he called *Season of Migration to the North* (African Writers Series 66). Tayeb Salih, who was on the BBC Arabic Service and spoke excellent English, rewrote the novel as they went along.

> Mustapha says that he will appease his race by liberating Africa with his penis. He exploits three women who fall in love with him and, two of whom, eventually commit suicide. He meets his match with a woman who cajoles him into marriage and eventually coaxes him to kill her.

The London *Observer* described it as 'an Arabian Nights in reverse'. There were more than twenty translations, most of which were made, rather than from the Beirut original, from Denys Johnson-Davies's English version on which he had worked so creatively with Tayeb Salih. Jill Neville said in the *Sunday Times*, 'I was hurled in a cauldron of morality, tensions and psychological bombshells with Tayeb Salih's classic.' In Paris, Claude Mauriac said: 'we have never read anything like this before, we who have read everything.'

Ousmane Sembène

The Senegalese novelist Ousmane Sembène was equally well known as a filmmaker. *God's Bits of Wood* (African Writers Series 63) is a realistic novel based on Sembène's personal experience of the 1947–8 strike on the great Dakar–Niger railway line, which held French colonial Africa together.

In *Xala* (African Writers Series no. 175), a businessman called

El Hadji Abdul Kajer Bey who, having bought a European bungalow for his bride, is on his wedding night struck with a *xala*; he is suddenly impotent. In this sharp satire Sembène shows the way in which the new African middle class were exploiting the ordinary people as the colonialists had done.

The Last of the Empire (African Writers Series 250) is a political novel set in Senegal. The President Mignane, who is quite obviously based on President Senghor, disappears.

Ferdinand Oyono

Ferdinand Oyono wrote two of the funniest books in the African Writers Series. *The Old Man and his Medal* (African Writers Series 39) deals with a single incident – the presentation of a medal by the French colonial authorities to Meka, an elderly African who had been a model colonial subject – and the events that immediately follow the ceremony. Through this simple narrative Oyono shows the nature of this colonial relationship and the folly of an African who abandons common sense and accepts white civilisation to the point of accepting its evaluation of himself.

Houseboy (African Writers Series 29) is in the form of a diary written by the houseboy, Toundi. Like Meka he is an innocent, fascinated and awed by the white world, and the story shows how his eyes are opened to the realities of this world. In the end, Toundi is destroyed because Europeans cannot endure the gaze of the man they have disillusioned. In spite of this ending *Houseboy* is a comic novel and Oyono's world is cheerful and there are entertaining scenes, such as where Toundi finds out about the Europeans' use of contraceptives.

While both books are very funny, they are also at the same time even more bitter than Mongo Beti's view of colonial life in Cameroun. Ferdinand Oyono became foreign minister, but if he had continued to write with such comedy, he would have been unable to continue his career.

Getting the African Writer Series into British bookshops and newspapers

Heinemann Educational Books relied on William Heinemann's bookshop representatives to sell the African Writers Series to British bookshops. One of my worst jobs was telling the reps about the African Writers Series after they had had a last lunch after a week-long sales conference. They far preferred selling the hardback novels by the South African author Wilbur Smith, with his long sweaty South African nights. They knew they ought not to look down on these books by African writers.

Fortunately, Paul Richardson, the history and politics editor, realised that they needed special marketing in bookshops. For instance, he managed to get a superb display in Heffer's bookshop in Trinity Street, Cambridge. For a month nobody could get down to the lower sales floor without walking through a display of the African Writers Series. I managed to get reviews into the London weeklies and monthlies such as the *Sunday Times* and *New Statesman*.

EIGHTEEN
Arab Authors

Cairo had the biggest book industry in Africa. In the African Writers Series we had several titles in translation by writers from the Arabic-speaking countries Egypt and Sudan. However, people in the Arab world looked down on Africans.

Denys Johnson Davies and I had launched Arab Authors as a parallel Heinemann series in time for the World of Islam Festival in London in 1976, which was funded by the oil boom. We commissioned new covers by artists and photographers from the Arab world. We produced a poster for the Arab Authors Series using a painting by the renowned Palestinian writer and PLO freedom fighter Ghassan Kanafani. His dramatic painting for a book of his stories was of a single horseman approaching with menace out of the desert.

Representatives from Penguin were full of admiration for the prominence of the Arab Authors Series in the booming bookshops of the Gulf states.

Denys Johnson-Davies explained that classical Arabic was a formal language understood right across the Arabic world, rather like Latin in monastic Europe.

There was disapproval among intellectuals of writing in contemporary colloquial Arabic, which was the language of the streets and offices and varied quite a lot from one side of the Arab world to the other. Denys Johnson-Davies reflected those dialects in his translations of speech in novels, stories, plays and poetry.

NINETEEN
Caribbean Writers Series

In the decade after the Second World War, quite a lot of novels from the Caribbean were being published by the leading London fiction publishers. As a result, there were published books available to be considered for the Caribbean Writers Series and only a couple of new titles were included. The African Writers Series had became far more successful because, as there were so few authors to reprint, new titles had to be published.

After his spell in South Africa, my grandfather John Currey had been made head of the Methodist Church on the Jamaica and Panama circuit, and my father visited his parents from Kingswood and Oxford.

Henry Swanzy, from an African Gold Coast family, started a programme called 'Caribbean Voices' on the BBC Colonial Service and regularly got my father, R. N. Currey, to do broadcasts and reviews for him. Henry Swanzy lived near my parents at Copford near Colchester. He was a clown who delighted in making children laugh. He had been married to an artist called Tirzah Garwood, the widow of the renowned artist Eric Ravilious who had been lost flying near Iceland in 1940.

In 1949, my mother Stella became close friends with Tirzah during her final struggle against cancer. After she died, Henry gave my parents Tirzah Garwood's picture of the three snowmen in the garden at Castle Hedingham. They gave it to Hal who lent it to the Dulwich Picture Gallery for an exhibition in 2024. A review in *The Week* (January 2025) said, 'Her final pictures produced as she lay dying in a nursing home are "wild and spry" and "self-reflective" in "an enchanting" show that is "a bright surprise from first to last".' Some years ago I used the three snowmen on my annual Christmas card. It is a delight for children of all ages.

Christmas cards

In 1946, my parents started to print their annual Christmas card with a poem on it by my father, R. N. Currey. When Oxford University Press sent me to South Africa in 1959 I started to send my own cards, which I designed, but also with a poem by R. N. Currey.

It was customary for printers and blockmakers to give publishers bottles of whisky at Christmas. I suggested that I would rather they forsook the whisky and instead printed my Christmas cards for free.

Sending Christmas cards is a cheerful way of keeping in touch with friends scattered around the world. By 2024 I had been sending cards for 65 years.

The department that women wanted to join

At a Heinemann Christmas party I was talking to Vicky Unwin, who had just been hired as a trainee after having completed her degree at Cambridge. When the managing director, Hamish MacGibbon, approached her and asked her for a cigarette, she said, 'only if you let me join James's African department'.

Apparently, mine was the department that women most wanted to join. I had a deputy called Penny Butler who was the same age as me and she used to come up to me and say, 'we've got trouble with the children.' The women said we ought to have another man in the department. Vicky had lived in East Africa when she was young because her Czech father had been sent there by the World Health Organization (WHO). When I left to set up James Currey Publishers, she took over running both the African Writers Series and my African list.

The Wednesday meeting

The rhythm of the week at Heinemann centred on the Wednesday meeting. Directors and editors could be sure they could get a decision within a week when needed.

There was a running duel between Keith Sambrook and the accountants who thought I was accepting too many new titles for the African Writers Series, the Caribbean Writers Series and the Arab Authors Series. After a bit, Alan Hill would say, 'well James! What does the old Chinua say?' He knew that I would have been in touch with young Chinua. 'Well James! You want to do it? Then do it!'

'The African Book Famine'

Michael Crowder coined the phrase, 'the African book famine'. It had started when the Nigerian foreign exchanges closed in April 1982 leaving the big publishers with container loads of books unpaid for; but these were mainly textbooks specifically written for the primary and secondary schools of English-speaking Africa.

The Nigerian oil boom then suddenly provided state governors with the wherewithal to order books in great quantities. At the same time there was also a huge increase in the rate of construction and, at the docks in Lagos, freighters full of concrete for building works would block the container ships full of books.

The Apapa wharves were jammed. A general nicknamed 'the Scorpion' made way for the concrete by using his armoured cars to tip containers of books off the wharves. The insurers insisted that the containers of sodden books still had to be delivered to the publishers. It was a dramatic sight when in the Heinemann warehouse yard in Jericho the container was tipped open and the water swept out bearing sodden copies of Kenneth Kaunda's *Zambia Shall be Free*.

It was a time of surprises. One Monday morning I received a telex from Heinemann Educational Books in Ibadan ordering one million cartons of colouring crayons for a state order for workbooks in eastern Nigeria. By lunchtime I had found a factory in Italy.

TWENTY

I Capture my Heinemann Titles

Heinemann taken over by the British Tyre and Rubber Company

In February 1964 Tillings, which then owned the Heinemann Group, was taken over by the conglomerate, the British Tyre and Rubber Company (BTR). Heinemann was told that it could only publish textbooks for secondary schools and that academic books were to be stopped. A new managing director called David Blunt was brought in to cut costs by closing departments and getting rid of directors. Keith Nettle had resigned and had not fought for redundancy payment; he had suffered a nervous breakdown before being offered the job of starting an educational department by the renowned publishers John Murray.

Blunt was deeply unpleasant. I was collecting something from his secretary's office and there were several women secretaries there. He walked in and announced, 'I have had a vasectomy!' In short, 'I am available!'

In September 1984 I was taken out to lunch by Richard Gale, the production director of Heinemann Educational Books, who warned me that I was next in Blunt's firing line. I was just off that afternoon to the annual African Studies conference, which was to take place at the new University of York. Sam Shepperson was professor of history at Edinburgh and an elder of African Studies. We had a cheerful drink together before I went to bed. I woke up at 3 o'clock in a state of delayed shock about what Richard had told me. By dawn, I had planned in detail how to set up James Currey Publishers. I took the train direct from York to Stevenage on Friday and walked into the kitchen at Walkern Mill and said to Clare, 'I don't think I have a future at Heinemann.' Clare said, 'I am glad you said it!'

As company secretary, Clare was to be a driving force behind James Currey Publishers and, in charge of finances, she enabled the firm to survive, thrive and move to Oxford.

Jimmy and Shirley Chesterman

William Heinemann had once hired Jimmy Chesterman to set up a paperback publishing imprint to rival Penguin and Pan, but when he put his plan to the board, he said, 'they rejected it! I walked out of the meeting! I walked out of publishing.'

We knew the Chestermans because both Clare and Jimmy's families had made fortunes for themselves in the steel town of Sheffield. Clares's family recycled gold and silver from the sweepings of goldsmiths and silversmiths from the floors of Birmingham workshop. Strangely enough, the Phipson branch of my family had run one of the those workshops.

All playing fields in the country used Chesterman rulers and tapes to measure tracks and jumps. Jimmy and Shirley Chesterman lived at Cutting Hill Farm, about four miles away from us, and Clare and I used to go riding with Shirley through stubble and mud.

The Chestermans once gave Clare a hot air balloon ride for a birthday present. Clare mentioned seeing a fox anxiously looking up at them as they floated over the countryside she and I knew so well from riding horses. Clare supported Shirley through Jimmy's faithlessness and the break up of their marriage, and I saw his randy behaviour at the dreaded Frankfurt Book Fair.

The best thing to come out of Frankfurt for me were 'Fishermen's Friends', the cough sweets I was offered while being interviewed by Deutsche Welle – the German World Service.

A hot-air balloon lands opposite Walkern Mill and the Miller's Cottage.

Pay my redundancy! Transfer my pension!

Jimmy Chesterman told me that I must insist that Heinemann pay my redundancy and that I transfer my pension funds. Clare and he agreed that I must not resign like Keith Nettle had done because that would mean that Heinemann would pay me nothing and be pleased to get rid of me.

On the Monday, Heinemann's chairman told me that I would only be able to publish 'a couple of volumes, like the UNESCO *General History of Africa* and a couple of titles in the African Writers Series such as the best-selling Ngugi'. I had been publishing about fifty titles a year, of which some fifteen or twenty literary titles were in the renowned African Writers Series, the newer Caribbean Writers Series and the Arab Authors Series. The new post-independence universities were producing academic scripts and African Studies were booming in American universities.

They had taken my job away. I demanded my redundancy. They refused. Clare, Tamsin and I went off for a planned holiday in Venice. I came back and again demanded my redundancy. It was refused. I flew off to Jamaica for a three-week Heinemann visit to Ian Randle with whom I had worked to set up the Heinemann Caribbean company. He loved my project and we spent most evenings at dinner going through management plans and my cash flow worksheets. He did not tell me was that he was planning to take over the Heinemann Caribbean company himself and, by going through my management plans, was learning about how to finance a small business – his firm was to become the outstanding publisher in the area.

Given a new publishing list

At a regular Wednesday directors' lunch, a member of staff said to David Blunt, Heinemann's new managing director: 'David. I have never cancelled an author's contract. How do you do it?' Blunt said, 'there's nobody in the London publishing world who has cancelled more contracts than I have!'

He then proceeded to tell us in detail how his chief aim was to get away with paying as little compensation as possible. A couple of days later I went into Blunt's office and said: 'David, you told us at lunch the other day how to cancel contracts. Why don't I ask my authors to assign their rights to my new company? That would save you the costs of cancelling their contracts.'

He promptly agreed on condition I repaid any costs that had already been incurred, such as the typesetting. I knew that the authors would be relieved that their books would still be published. In a couple of sentences I had been given a new publishing list.

Should I buy my Heinemann backlist?

At one stage I thought that it would be valuable to make Heinemann an offer for the stock of my African and Caribbean titles. As a result, in early 1985, Keith Sambrook and I carefully costed how much I should offer. Heinemann refused because 'I had already got away with too much.' In retrospect, I eventually realised that it would have been a mistake because it would have meant taking over stale, slow-selling stock. We did, however, take over Heinemann's *African Literature Today*, a subscription journal producing four issues a year. We turned it into a book and from the fifth issue onwards, gave each annual volume a title focused on a single topic.

It was an inspired change because, fortunately, for about £30, Richard Gale was able to sell us the unsold stock at only 5p a copy. This gave us the wherewithal to commission new volumes of which there are now well over thirty. Academic journals were booming.

Terence Ranger, Colin Leys and James Currey Publishers

When I arrived at Oxford University Press in Cape Town in 1959, there had been much talk about the African visit of Alan Hill from Heinemann. He had found two important academic advisers who were to be central to the growth of my African Studies list when I joined him. One was Colin Leys, principal of Kivukoni College near Dar es Salaam. His *Rise and Fall of Development Theory*, which I published in 1996 when he had returned to Balliol College, was to be one of our most seminal books. The other was Terence Ranger, who was teaching at the University of Rhodesia and Nyasaland. Terry Ranger remembered visiting me in my Heinemann office in Bedford Square in September 1984 and noticing that, South African style, I always left my office door open. He said, 'you got up and closed the office door, so I knew things were serious.'

His latest book, *Peasant Consciousness and Guerrilla War in Zimbabwe* (1985), had been edited and was already at the galley proof stage. I told him that I was starting my own company and asked him if I could take over the publication of his book. He looked at me very seriously and said, 'as long as it's out by September 1985!' His agreement was vital.

He told me later that some academics had told him that, while they admired what I was doing, they felt at this stage in their careers an established publisher like Cambridge University Press would look better on their CVs. Terry replied that it was up to them, but that he had sold his rights to my new company.

On one Thursday each month, he used to travel up from Oxford to our flat in London where he would have dinner with us and spend the night. We would devote the next morning to going through any history and politics manuscripts that might have arrived in the interim, and deciding which to send out for reports, which to reject, and which to accept.

When in 1987 he became Rhodes Professor of Race Relations and African History at Oxford, his inaugural lecture in the Examination Schools was turned into a celebration of the establishment of African history at Oxford.

At his retirement dinner at St Antony's, he said that I was the only editor with whom he had published all his own books – when I was with Oxford University Press, with Heinemann and then with James Currey Publishers. We had also published many of his edited collections of work on Zimbabwean and African studies.

Alison and Busby and Currey =A&B&C

During that autumn of 1984 I approached Clive Alison and Margaret Busby who were radical literary publishers of Caribbean and African authors. They were known as A&B. I suggested I join them to create a publisher of African and Caribbean academic books called A&B&C. It was a nice idea. It was decided we would move into a room in A&B's office and see how it worked out.

On a gloomy Monday morning on 12 January 1985, Ingrid Crewdson and I loaded up the station wagon in Islington with furniture and files and drove down to Allison and Busby in Noel Street in Soho. Clive Allison quite rightly looked embarrassed when we arrived to occupy a room in their narrow office building and to establish A&B&C as the academic wing of this enterprising general and literary publisher A&B. The nine members of staff had revolted and said that there was not enough space for them as it was. They were right.

We drove back to Islington and started our business in our basement flat right there at 72b – the b stood for basement – Thornhill Square in Islington.

Being only a 12-minute bike ride away from the School for Oriental and African Studies (SOAS), anybody coming through London from Africa, America or indeed Britain could easily be met and entertained at 54 (b) Thornhill Square underneath our friends Ian and Lydia Wright. Ian, who was only two years older than me, was a friend at school and Oxford. He had started as a film critic and was on his way to becoming the managing editor of the *Guardian*. I went to meet him at the *Guardian* office on 23 October 1962 when the Cuban missile crisis almost brought us into a third world war.

Hijacking an office at night

Towards Christmas 1984, Richard Helm, who was the son of a friend, and a fellow student from Vancouver moved the Heinemann overseas editorial department from Bedford Square to our flat in Thornhill Square in gentrifying Islington. Bedford Square at ten o'clock in the evening was bathed in streetlight. The filing cabinet had a whole publishing business within its four drawers. The boxes of manuscripts were the future of our business. Fortunately, nobody asked us if we were robbers.

Publisher's lunches

Lunch paid for by the publisher is a useful part of the working day. Wine bars were a new fashion and near Heinemann's West End office there was an atmospheric one under a French wine shop in Shepherd Market. A favourite Italian restaurant was in a basement in the street on the other side of Brown's Hotel.

Alan Hill had said that, since I was a director, Heinemann would pay for my membership of a London club. A Wilson cousin, who was the head of the Public Records Office, offered to put me up for the Reform Club, and when I declined said, 'what about the Athenaeum?' I explained that since half my authors were women, I would be unable to entertain them in a men's club. In any case, I did not go for the formality or for the comfort food.

I had to work out three months' notice until Christmas at Heinemann Educational Books. This was useful as Heinemann paid for our lunches when I took authors out to tell them what was happening and ask if I could take over their manuscripts. My boss Keith Sambrook, the overseas director, was a quiet ally who delighted in talking through the detailed plans. I asked my editorial colleague Ingrid Crewdson whether, if I could negotiate the payment of her redundancy by Heinemann, she would join Clare's and my venture. We paid her a salary while for the first three years we did not pay ourselves. We took out insurance to cover illness, as absence from the office would cost us dear, but it did not cover unplanned maternity leave for Ingrid.

Our new routine in Islington was to provide lunch at the office or in the garden. American authors would arrive after an overnight flight thinking it will be good to recover over lunch with James and Clare. After the author had left, I would put my feet up on the sofa and then work through the evening until I pulled out my mattress at midnight. Clare would work for three days a week, and spend two nights in the basement.

'How exciting to be a publisher!' *'Not half as exciting as working for CAB!'*

Clare had given up a paid supervisor's job at the Citizens Advice Bureau in Stevenage. People would say, 'how exciting to be a publisher!' and she replied 'not half as exciting as working at the CAB.' Clare had had only limited freelance publishing experience and was modest about her organisational skills. It became essential she worked for the company, though we both feared it might put too much strain on our marriage. We were walking down Thornhill Square one day when she said, 'what books do you want me to do?' My answer shocked her, 'the account books!' She handled the family finances and her family shares in Rowntree and the Sheffield Smelting Company and it was these investments that enabled us to risk starting a publishing company. We calculated that we could afford to lose up to £80,000 over three years. She had paid back ahead of time the money we had borrowed from Barclays to convert Walkern Mill.

The bank manager at Hitchin immediately agreed to give our new business an overdraft facility of £25,000. Clare hated drawing on it at all. We only once had a cheque bounce because, without telling her, Barclays had halved the facility to £12,500 because she had not used the overdraft enough. Cash flow was no problem. The printers gave us three months to pay and the United States university treasuries paid our book invoices dead on time. These margins meant that our copies of the books had been paid for by the time they went into stock. I spent a lot of time filling in cash flow sheets in pencil so that I could rub out the figures if I had made a mistake. Keith Sambrook was always available to go through the month's figures, which he enjoyed.

I was quite frightened of setting up a business on our own

I was nervous about setting up a business on my own and took every opportunity to look for an established London publisher who would take over the African Writers Series with me, as editorial director, providing the new books and authors. I had detailed discussions with David Godwin about William Heinemann taking over the African Writers Series with me from Heinemann Educational Books. He thought it a splendid idea but then told me that he personally was on the way to joining Secker & Warburg and then Jonathan Cape – he was to become the literary agent that writers most wanted to have represent them.

I had discussions with other publishing friends about them taking over the series with me as editor. Hugo Brunner had joined Oxford University Press on the same day as me and had recently bought Chatto & Windus. I was also approached, on his own initiative, by Martin Spencer of Manchester University Press.

Christopher Hurst was a one-man specialist publisher of area studies in the Third World who took every chance to help us. Clare always rang him first for advice. He worked from an office in the Africa Centre in King Street.

He recommended us to his distributors, J. M. Dent & Sons, who were the publishers of the Everyman Classics and who had a substantial warehouse in Letchworth Garden City. They provided for selected small publishers what the Americans call 'fulfilment' – namely storing books, invoicing out to bookshops, and collecting money owed. They were the leaders in subcontracting services. This was most important. We had been given the books, but we needed to get them to the bookshops.

TWENTY-ONE
James Currey Publishers Founded

James Currey Publishers starts on 12 January 1985

James Currey Publishers started on 12 January 1985. Clare and I set it up to publish academic books on Africa, the Caribbean and the Third World. We set out to publish for the three continents of Europe, America and Africa. We had to make co-publishing work if we were to survive. Some people said 'how brave!', which really meant 'how foolish!'

Longman, OUP, Macmillan, Nelson and Heinemann had all dropped out of academic publishing on Africa. Only Cambridge University Press was continuing its distinguished African Studies Series in this period of debt. OUP had had a proud record in the 1960s with its Clarendon Press African Studies Series. Julian Rea's history of publishing with Longman, especially on West Africa, was enviable. Heinemann had become the most popular, with in excess of 250 Penguin coloured paperbacks in the African Writers Series of novels, plays and poetry. Also, Heinemann had built a distinguished African studies list.

Faxes pour in from across the world

We had found a plain, elegantly battered chest in a junk shop in the Caledonian Road. On the top of it we placed our wonderful new acquisition, a fax. I used to pull out a mattress to sleep on the floor next to it. At 3 a.m. one morning some thirty sheets started angrily pouring over me. I had to look to see who it was from. It was from California from a Jewish publisher attacking the manuscript *Cultural Forces in World Politics*, which I had offered him from the renowned Ali Mazrui, whose Islamic family had ruled Mombasa since the sixteenth century. Ali Mazrui provocatively offered to add a chapter on the *intifada* – the popular Palestinian rising on the West Bank. John Watson's Heinemann Inc. happily took it.

Ali Mazrui was chosen one year by the BBC to deliver the renowned Reith Lectures. Ali made sure that we, rather than the usual Cambridge University Press, published *The African Condition*. The Reith Lectures are still an annual event in 2025.

Co-publish with American university presses

It takes a lot of time and money to get academic manuscripts edited for typesetting. It is essential to build up the print run so as to spread the start-up costs over as many copies as possible.

In my 17 years at Heinemann, I built up close friendships and co-publishing partnerships with the few editors in the United States with specialist lists in African studies at the university presses of California, Ohio and Indiana. John Gallman at Indiana University Press said he saw me as the scout who brought in the best African books for his list. His father had been US ambassador in Pretoria and, for a couple of years, he had gone to the Pretoria High School. After having crossed over to Britain on the very same weekend as the Americans went into the Gulf, he stayed with us in rural Hertfordshire and I, in turn, stayed with him on his farm in Indiana where he cropped alfalfa lucerne feed.

At the Nashville African Studies Association meeting in 2000, I was given a special award in recognition of my outstanding services in the field of African studies; this was the only time that they had given such an award to a publisher. I had already received an award from the Canadian ASA and was later to get a similar one

JAMES CURREY PUBLISHERS FOUNDED

Lynn Taylor with James Currey after he was awarded the African Studies Award at Nashville 2000.

(Left to right) James Currey, Chinua Achebe, Doug Killam, Christine Achebe, Clare Currey at Bard College, November 2000.

from the African Studies Association of the United Kingdom (ASAUK). Later, I was enstooled on an Ashanti chair by the Pan-African Writers Association in Ghana.

In November 2000, we spent a week at the Achebe conference at Bard College in Upstate New York. Because I realised Chinua Achebe was under-recognised in America, I wrote and published a book called *Africa Writes Back* (2008) on the African Writers Series and launch of African literature. It covered eight of the outstanding writers I had published and surveyed the literature from eastern, western and southern Africa. Professor Bernth Lindfors claimed it was 'worth the price of the book for the chapter on "Publishing Dambudzo Marechera" alone.'

Each year the African Studies Association (ASA) was in a different city and would occupy one, two or three hotels, all of which would invariably have a swimming pool. Once, when Clare and I were in the jacuzzi, another couple attending the conference asked us for our names. When we told them what they were, the wife replied: 'Oh! You have just rejected my book! You wrote me a very kind rejection letter!' I then told her that turning down manuscripts was of deep concern to me and that my mother had been a successful writer of novels and short stories. I also told her that my father who had been a poet used to go downstairs to collect the post at 7.30 each morning and that they would then sit up in bed to read the rejection letters and decide which journals and publishers to try next.

For me, the most important co-publisher in America was Heinemann itself, which John Watson ran from New England as Heinemann Inc. Ever since 1974 I had, with difficulty, got Heinemann to pay for me to go to the African Studies Association (ASA) conferences. When Clare and I started James Currey Publishers in 1984, John said, 'you can't afford not to come to the ASA!' He then invited us to display our books at one end of his stand. Everybody looked for the Heinemann stand. Once, a black American academic stood in the middle of the central aisle and shouted 'Where is James Currey?' We had become the African studies publisher of choice.

JAMES CURREY PUBLISHERS FOUNDED

Co-publish with presses from end to end of Africa

We set out to get as many copies into Africa as possible, but in postcolonial times there were foreign exchange problems and I often had to resort to barter. For instance, we built up a mutually advantageous relationship with Baobab Press in Zimbabwe whereby it would edit and typeset and we would print the book and pay for it with finished copies printed in England. The African order was important for an author who had worked in a country for many years and had friends who longed to read what had been found out about them. When I published my book *Africa Writes Back*, it was first in conjunction with Witwatersrand University Press for the Cape Town Book Fair, then with six other publishers elsewhere in Africa, and then with Ohio University Press. We then published for the Commonwealth and the rest of the world.

Many people were surprised and disappointed that I was not going to try to rival the African Writers Series – they felt I ought to take on and show up Heinemann and BTR. However, we had made such a success of publishing and marketing the series that it would have been be suicidal to try to rival Heinemann. Go for the gap! There was a postcolonial boom in African studies in the United States. African studies and the study of African literature were what was exciting. I knew we could make enough of a margin to survive if we presold half the print run to an academic publisher for the United States and Canada. We had to test the patience of authors while we got detailed academic reports and negotiated co-publishing arrangements for their books.

'You may make your fortune!'

Clare's brother Chris Wilson contacted a friend from Queen's College Oxford who was now an investment banker. He kindly

JAMES CURREY PUBLISHERS FOUNDED

Dennis Brutus speaks at the launch of James Currey's Africa Writes Back *Cape Town Bookfair 2008.*

invited me to his penthouse office overlooking London near Waterloo. I had prepared a detailed business plan. His leading question was 'are you setting up this business to continue your career or to make a fortune?' I blushed and said it was to continue my career. He said 'you may make your fortune!'

Publish in Islington: Thornhill Square and Caledonian Road

On setting up an office for our new business, we decided that, at least temporarily, we would locate ourselves in our basement flat in Islington and then see what else we could find. Christopher Hurst had said that a publisher had to be in central London to survive. I tended to agree. I went to discuss possibilities with Tom Rosenthal at André Deutsch of renting a room in their offices, although he could charge a steep rent in Great Russell Street round the corner from the British Museum. André Deutsch had been involved with John Nottingham and the establishment of the pioneering East African Publishing House (EAPH) in Nairobi and the African Universities Press in Nigeria.

Investment and ownership and survival

I was nervous about our ability to survive on our own and during that winter was tempted by various approaches that were made to us about investment and ownership. Zed Books was located in a red-light street in pre-gentrified King's Cross. In the first fortnight, I invited Roger van Zwannenburg and Robert Molteno round for lunch. Roger said that Robert could not come. In fact, he had not passed on my invitation and clearly this was because, by the end of lunch, it had become apparent that he wanted personally to offer to invest in us. He said that the worst thing he had done with Zed Books was to set it up as a workers' collective. In 1987, he was to take over Pluto Press.

There was also an approach from one of the founders and owners of the blue news sheet *Africa Confidential*. He said that since its foundation in 1960, they had accumulated a mass of information about emerging Africa and we both saw the possibilities of drawing on that for a series of reference books on Africa.

A totally surprising proposition came from Martin Spencer, the publisher at Manchester University Press (MUP), which was the only university press of substance in England outside Oxford and Cambridge. He and I had admired one another as rivals when he had worked on Africa for Longman. MUP had long published for the Rhodes–Livingstone Institute near the Victoria Falls in Zambia. Martin Spencer was an Africa enthusiast and suggested he set up James Currey Publishers as an MUP imprint. We would maintain our identity. For instance, he visualised a James Currey section on tinted paper bang in the centre of the MUP catalogue so that nobody could miss it. MUP would share investment and share margins. We would produce the books and MUP would market them. It was a flattering suggestion and I worked enthusiastically at proposals with him. We had discussions in London and then with the accounts and marketing departments in Manchester. The more figure work we did the more we reluctantly agreed that there was unlikely to be enough in the margins for both of us. However, these discussions warmed up a cold spring and made me feel that the imprint was wanted and had a future.

Denmark

One of my authors, Holger Bernt Hansen, was doing a lot of work in Uganda for Danida, the brand name for the Danish government's development and humanitarian programmes. At that time, Uganda was still recovering from Idi Amin's dictatorship, and *Uganda Now* was the title of his first book, though we published several others of his as well. Holga Bernt Hansen, also ran conferences on Uganda at a folk high school outside Copenhagen. Once when I arrived back from such a conference, Tamsin was bathing her daughter Martha, and I went on and on so much about my visit to Denmark that my granddaughters Martha and Hattie have called me 'Denmark' instead of 'Grandpa'.

Finland

Finland had always been very special to me. My Uncle Hal's wife Mairie had lost her first husband in the war against the Russians during the winter of 1940. My cousin Alice, their daughter, had got me invited to give a lecture at Helsinki University. It was the biggest audience I ever had and people were sitting right up to the back rows. She also arranged for me to attend a seminar with Finnish writers.

JAMES CURREY PUBLISHERS FOUNDED

Tamsin telling her father about her new Marimekko nightdress brought from Finland by Hal and Marie.

Cousin Alice Martin in Finland.

JAMES CURREY PUBLISHERS FOUNDED

On another visit to Helsinki, Clare and I were sitting on the great wide steps of the Post Office waiting for the airport bus to arrive and, for the first time, we noticed that every young man seemed to be looking at their Nokia mobile phone. The Nokia company had started in Finland as far back as in the mid-nineteenth century and was first of all known for manufacturing what we would call Wellington boots. Nokia had become the Gutenberg of our time.

Clare is stricken with cancer

When Clare was diagnosed with terminal cancer, she and I were given great comfort and care at Maggie's Care Centre just across the road from the Churchill Hospital in Oxford. I could work there all day and go across regularly to talk to Clare. She was moved when her conditioned worsened, spending her final days in the wonderful Sobell House Hospice. Clare died on the 26 April 2016 Hal, Tamsin and I were seated round the table at Thames Street when we received the news. My memory of the next few days has gone.

The African Aids Epidemic (2006)

John Iliffe, a history professor at Cambridge, chose to use us rather than Cambridge University Press because he knew we would get the book out quickly. We sold co-editions to Ohio University Press and to Juta's imprint Double Storey Books in Cape Town. Everybody needed to have information fast on this desperate plague. An important case study was Sandra Wallman's *Kampala Women Getting By: Wellbeing in the Time of Aids*. Another was *Letting Them Die* by Catherine Campbell, which is about a project in a South African mining township that tried and failed to reduce the rate of HIV infection.

New series

Two series brought in a wide range of work from both sides of Africa – the Eastern African Series on countries from Ethiopia to Mozambique and a West African Series. There were others on the 'Social History of Africa' and 'Readings in ...', which were recent documents selected for textbook use.

Professor Wendy James, who was married to my publishing partner Douglas Johnson, brought us into a new series called 'World Anthropology' and co-published with the American School for Advanced Research Press.

African Issues

African Issues were a collection of books on any African subject in the humanities presented in a Penguin/Pelican format. *Africa Works* was a particular success. Douglas Johnson's *The Root Causes of Sudan's Civil Wars* was one of the founding titles in 2003. Alex de Waal's *Famine Crimes: Politics and the Disaster Relief Industry in Africa* (2007) reveals how governments can create a famine to exert control. *Congo–Paris* (2000) paints a vivid picture of the fashions of the transnational traders in Paris. African Issues was a great and original idea.

The UNESCO General History of Africa

UNESCO commissioned historians from around the world to produce an eight-volume history, which would be published in five languages. I got University of California Press to put in a joint bid with Heinemann to co-publish the eight volumes of the English language edition.

JAMES CURREY PUBLISHERS FOUNDED

James Currey in Libya where UNESCO was celebrating its eight-volume General History of Africa, *which President Gaddafi had funded.*

I was rung up and told that the francophones in the UNESCO Council were attacking our bid, which was taking place in Paris. I straightaway flew to Paris and as I entered the Council chamber everybody stood up. I had saved the project by coming to Paris. The funding came from Colonel Gaddafi in Libya.

The Libyans later had a UNESCO conference in a military camp of marquees in the desert area surrounding the city of Sirte, which was a memorable event for me. When Gaddafi appeared in our tent he was flanked by two giant female guards.

African film

Francophone West Africa produced a remarkable number of outstanding filmmakers. Ousmane Sembène from Senegal was both a filmmaker and writer of fiction and we published a translation of his *Les Bouts du Bois du Dieu – God's Bit of Wood* (African Writers Series no. 163) – a novel about an historic strike on the great French railway line across West Africa. In *Africa Shoots Back* (2003), Melissa Thackway discusses the most memorable films from francophone Africa. Josef Gugler, with *African Film* (2003), wrote a handbook for African film lovers. *Black and White in Colour* (2007) concentrates on historical themes, such as the slave trade, imperialism and anti-colonial resistance. *Man and Masculinities in African Film and Fiction* (2008) was another title.

Oral literature

Ruth Finnegan at the newly founded Open University wrote *The Oral and Beyond: Doing Things with Words in Africa* (2007). Her provocative conclusion was that it was time to abandon the long-entrenched image of Africa as 'the oral continent' and to adopt a more critical comparative attitude to 'oral literature'.

JAMES CURREY PUBLISHERS FOUNDED

Basil Davidson

Basil Davidson, who had been parachuted into Tito's headquarters in Yugoslavia during the Second World War, was a well-known war correspondent. After the war he worked with guerrilla groups in Africa. We republished his *Black Star: Kwame Nkrumah*, along with *The African Slave Trade* and his cleverly titled *The Black Man's Burden* (1994). When he rang and offered me *The Search for Africa*, I said I would surely be unable to afford the advance. He said the American advance was so substantial that he could afford to go without one. He said he wanted me to publish anyway as we would get the book into Africa.

Once, when Clare and I were visiting the Davidsons in the Mendips in Somerset, our Morris Convertible broke down and the Automobile Association (AA) said it would have to take the car back to our garage in Hertfordshire. Watching the tall, elegant Lieutenant-Colonel Davidson commanding the loading of the Morris Convertible onto the AA lorry was a memorable sight.

D-Day at 75

The radio was full of reminiscences to celebrate VE-Day on 8 and 9 May 2019 when Radio Oxford asked me for my recollections of being the age of nine at the time. From what I recall, there was no announcement at school, and I only heard about it later when some schoolboys told me in Beverley Road after school. I cannot remember my mother reacting at all. My father was away in India at the time where he had been seconded to the *Times of India* in Bombay to write pamphlets for the British troops to ensure that they expected the war against the Japanese to go on for more years. I feel sure she feared the same. In fact, the war went on until August 1945 when the United States dropped the atom bomb on Hiroshima and again two days later on Nagasaki.

Joanna Cacanas

The Holburne Museum in Bath arranged a visit to Vienna leaving on 8 February 2018. Joanna wanted me to go with her and booked two neighbouring rooms in the very grand hotel. On Tresco that July, we shared the great double bed looking out to Bishop's Rock. This was the first time I had been to the Isles of Scilly since Clare's death.

Joanna and I were together very often during the first half of 2022. In January, she accompanied me to a grand party hosted by Clare's brother Lyn at Emmanuel College in Cambridge. She spent time with me by the river in Oxford each month, and we took every chance we could to listen to Bach, especially in the New College chapel on the first Sunday of each month. She believed. I did not, but I delighted in helping her do her work as a churchwarden of the church in Swainswick. There were memorial meetings for Robert Molteno, as well as for Mary Tinker, who had worked with us at the firm.

The Oxford Literary Festival of March 2022 included a session on me and, in June that year, a documentary film was made called *Rediscovering James Currey*.

On 24 June I had an awful night and realised I had Covid. I rang for an ambulance at 7.06 but thankfully the doctor on the telephone decided not to send me to the John Radcliffe Hospital with its risk of infection from other diseases. He thankfully prescribed five days of self-isolation.

On 19 August 2022, Tamsin drove me to Bath to stay in the big house with Joanna's daughter Rachel where Joanna was still in bed after Covid. On Monday 22 August, I sat with Joanna in her wheelchair outside on the street by the green garage door and neighbours stopped in their cars to talk to her. On Tuesday I was urged by her daughters Lucy, Rachel and Zoe not to go back to Oxford. Joanna was downstairs in bed in the living room at the top of some steps. On Wednesday evening there were visitors who had

Joanna Cacanas shows Hal and Wycliffe Stutchbury her family doll's house.

gone for a walk down the wonderful hillside garden below the house. I came back inside to find that Joanna had swung round out of bed with one foot hanging down. I shouted down the garden to the visitors: HELP! HELP! HELP!

On Thursday morning the district nurse administered a 'driver' of drugs to reduce the pain. I did not realise that Joanna was dying. On Friday 26 August I sat with her for a while and held her hand and then went outside to the street. At 11.00 I was quietly told that she had gone. I went upstairs to avoid the undertakers.

Tamsin and I were seated below the pulpit at her funeral in Swainswick church. Her daughter Zoe Elliot spoke about how the village of some 250 souls had felt such delight in Joanna's joy and originality. Joanna had apparently spoken to her about our relationship and had referred to me 'her boyfriend'. It was a new idea to me that she considered me 'quite a catch'. I just took our coming and going as friends and lovers as natural. During the lockdown we had slipped into a 'bubble' between Oxford and Bath, which is hopefully what I would have told the police had we been stopped. She is buried in the churchyard beside her late husband

JAMES CURREY PUBLISHERS FOUNDED

George. She made a lovely and exceedingly elegant drawing of the church, which I used as a Christmas card one year. Clare, Joanna, George and I had been close friends ever since we first met at university. I am the only survivor. Clare died on 26 April 2016; George on 23 August 2016; and Joanna on 26 August 2022. Since Joanna lost George and I lost Clare within months of each other in 2016, we took to staying with each other more and more frequently. She described our last six years together as a 'bonus'. We discussed whether we should marry, but decided on a gentle continuation as friends, each with our own families and houses. She feared that my family would consider that I was not being true to Clare.

The Roberts side of Joanna's family were military people and her Uncle Bob's portrait – and he was none other than the famous Lord Roberts of Kandahar – hung on the guestroom wall of her family home.

Lord Roberts had taken part in the 1920 equestrian events at the Olympics where his British team of one hundred military horsemen won silver medal. George Cacanas's English mother had married a Greek general who had been killed when the Italians invaded Bosnia in 1940.

George Cacanas was a student at Worcester College when Joanna was studying at the Ruskin School of Art in Oxford. I am very fond of her paintings. Some of them are on the first floor of my house in Thames Street, including a relatively recent one of our terrace viewed from the other side of the river.

For one half-term holiday, Clare booked us into a flat overlooking the front of Bath Abbey, with its famous ladders of angels. Joanna and George, who were living in Bath at that time, invited us to Upper Swainswick House, which was a magnificent property she had inherited from one of her aunts. Given that Swainswick House was at least double the width of a classic Bath limestone house, it was too large for their needs, so she and George decided to live in the stables on the other side of the courtyard.

Joanna had also inherited a dramatic four-storey doll's house, which she delighted in showing to us.

JAMES CURREY PUBLISHERS FOUNDED

A yen to keep a penguin

In a letter from Cape Town to her parents, Ruth and Henry Wilson, on 18 February 1963 Clare wrote:

> James has got a great yen to keep a penguin but I don't think we live near enough to the sea. He thinks he could take it down to the sea each day (which part of the apartheid bus, 'White' or 'Non-European', do you think it would qualify for?) and put it in the sea to catch fish and then bring it home in the evening. He also suggested keeping it in the washing machine. I wondered if it could be trained to empty the rubbish bin but we both fear that it might not be able to climb the stairs. (Orange covered Penguin Books were founded in the year 1936 which was the year of Clare's and James's birth.)

Boulders Beach in the Cape where we swam among penguins.

TWENTY-TWO
Lockdown for the Plague

Saturday 21 March 2020: the spring equinox

This date marked a starting point for the arrival of the coronavirus in the Thames Valley. My terrace of 17 houses, backing onto Thames Street and just upriver from Folly Bridge, has neighbourly front yards overlooking the river. Since people only started 'self-isolating' that week, informal groups began to exchange news over their low walls. They are a heterogeneous and interesting group, with representatives from Australia, New Zealand, California and South Africa. There is a Norwegian conducting research into building materials and an Australian medical economist who can put figures on cholera in Oxford in the mid-nineteenth century. There is Sonya who was on the Taiwan desk of the Australian Foreign Service – now Taiwan is the computer chip capital of the world and in frontline danger from China. Then there are Karin Fremer, a Swedish book designer for Thames & Hudson, and Joseph Chamberlin, a filmmaker for BBC TV4 and other TV broadcasters, and me, a publisher of books on Africa and the Caribbean.

Everybody had more time to fill and less time to worry about being willing to spend too much time talking. One could slip into a group and slip off again without ceremony. Philip Clarke, the Australian economist next door, is a dedicated cook and rang one Friday evening to say that he had over-produced his rack of lamb and would I join them. Sonya Kelly says he always buys too much.

My grandfather J. P. Martin's missionary box on the front stoep, which I had repainted Oxford blue, was of immediate use for food and parcel deliveries. It was marvellous that the post continued to be delivered and that the pillar boxes were not sealed.

To avoid handling the locked post boxes outside each house, the postman would toss the packs of letters onto the doorstep if the door was open. I failed to figure out how the postman had managed to open the latch to the porch and put the post into Clare's electric bike basket. He must have somehow slid the letters over the gap at the top of the glass door.

Stephen Hugh-Jones and Isis

On a Saturday morning in 2020 I opened *The Economist* and found a tribute to the originator of its Johnson column, Stephen Hugh-Jones:

> The founder of this column had just died on 28 February 2020. He was an extraordinary character at *The Economist* – long, lean, waspish and a self-appointed menace to facile consensus. His theatrical interventions tended to come at Monday editorial meetings where sitting on the floor with his back to the editor's he would shout exclamations such as 'Baloney'. A stubborn legend pursued Stephen Hugh-Jones that he threw a typewriter at the window in his rage, intending to but failing to break the glass.

As I mentioned earlier in this book, Stephen Hugh-Jones had featured large in my undergraduate days, especially in his role as the editor of *Isis*.

One of my closest friends at that time was Roger Pethybridge, with whom I had run the Oxford International Committee conferences. He, like many of the others from that time, had been on the Russian course.

He had also been at the World Health Organization in Geneva where he was aide-de-camp to Russian Chairman Graschenkov. He was shocked by the corruption in the UN and said that his job consisted largely of running errands like buying presents for the chairman's mother in Russia.

Learning about computers

Wednesday 1 April 2020. My Casio wrist watch played an April Fool's joke on me by telling me that this morning was 4 April 2020. It had reduced my March to 28 days, as it had done for February. I asked Sonya Kelly my neighbour if it was Wednesday from her balcony next door. She told me that I had better not try that one on Joanna in Bath.

On the same day I also experienced my first attempted telephone scam. At 12.45 a posh lady at the Co-operative Bank rang me up to say that a sum of around £70,000 had been taken from my account. I told her she must tell me this in writing and that I had closed my account, which only had about £1100 in it, which I had sent to HSBC. I was very cross and told the lady from the Co-operative Bank far too much. It showed how putting the phone down without a word to unsolicited phone calls from Bangalore is safest and all you need do. They are apparently trying to get your numbers so they can raid your account.

Tamsin got my Canon printer cartridges delivered to the blue box on my stoep. After three days, I got Duncan the computer expert from Buntingford to appear like magic via TeamViewer (a green cross on the screen) and get me to do the things necessary to unjam my machine.

With the great Covid crisis still raging, and without coming to see me, Duncan was, in effect, to give me two computer tutorials online. I had to stop him moving the cursor and instead get him to instruct me on how to move it. There seem to be several names for what appears to me to be the same feature of a computer – namely 'Window', 'Screen' and 'Menu'. I have already given up my efforts to learn how to pay online and he says I can still give a him an archaic cheque. The window cleaners have already taken my equally old-fashioned £15 of cash. On Saturday 2 May I have a valuable Zoom instruction morning arranged for me by Hal.

Palm Sunday, 5 April 2020

I decided not to cycle for exercise. Since the first-floor front room was alight with sun, I set about sorting out the books that Joanna had carried down from the top front bedroom, to stack in the new walls of bookshelves on the first floor. It is becoming a library. I am slowly recovering from the bicycle accident I had on the Plain when I was flung across the bonnet of a car coming out of Cowley Road. I can now carry books and place them on the shelves. When Joanna was herself bringing them down I had found it too painful to lift heavy books to the top shelves.

In the late afternoon I had a good catch-up telephone call with my cousin Alice in Helsinki, who is also under Covid restrictions.

The struggle to get your future wives to marry you

On 27 April 2020, in response to having received a copy of our book, Rose Luce wrote: 'I loved the photograph of Clare near the beginning of *From Sharpeville to Rivonia*. What an interesting story. Oddly enough you and Richard have a lot in common in the struggle to get your future wives to marry you. Also, neither Clare nor I wanted to live abroad, you in South Africa, us in Kenya.' In 2024 Richard, as Lord Luce, was put in charge of finding a new Archbishop of Canterbury after the resignation of Justin Welby.

Banging in support of workers in Covid front line

As the sun was setting on the evening of Friday 3 April 2020, everybody went out onto the streets to shout and bang saucepans in support of the health and transport workers who had so valiantly been risking their lives on the front line of the Covid pandemic. We shouted in support of pharmacy workers risking infection over the counter as people were being turned away from A&E because all the hospital beds and corridors were already full of cases.

Lockdown forecasts

Forecasts for the expected length of the lockdown were being increased daily – first ten days, followed by three weeks, and then a first mention of a six-month lockdown. BBC Four became locked in a battle with Minister of Health Matt Hancock about the delay in testing for a virus that three months earlier few people knew existed. People were getting confused over the differences between antibodies and tests – one with a swab, the other with a machine. It turns out that, allegedly, Hancock has been making a fortune for himself and his friends by selling protective clothing for nurses.

In 1947, I remember reading about the military facility at Porton Down in a children's magazine. It is now the centre for the development of a coronavirus vaccine.

White van in river

On 18 April 2020, while talking to my neighbour Joe Cunningham, he got me to turn round. A white van was lodged on a shoal on the other side of the river. It must have been driven with intent to knock down our carpark post and plunge into the river. A man with a beard on the opposite bank jumped in and got the driver out of his van. At least it provided us with some good entertainment for lockdown.

Virtual May Morning online

On Friday 1 May 2022, there was an electronic surprise when the Oxford Preservation Society presented May Morning online. It meant that one could now see the choristers singing on top of the tower for the first time ever.

An explorer survives coronavirus

On Tuesday 5 May 2022, Radio 4 gave an account of a man being wheeled out into the sunshine under open skies, with flowers growing all around him and gradually becoming aware of the reawakening of his consciousness. It was only then that he was told that he had been unconscious for 49 days, during which time he had very nearly died of Covid twice. We then learnt that this man was none other than Robin Hanbury-Tenison, the explorer we had met when Clare, Hal, Tamsin and I first visited Tresco in 1972.

The roaring boy Roy Campbell

Before the war, my father R. N. Currey had been friends with another South African poet, Roy Campbell, and he often met him in London. Despite Campbell's attacks against racism and his angry rejection of Sir Oswald Mosley's efforts to recruit him into the British Union of Fascists, in his native South Africa, Campbell continued to be labelled a fascist and left out of poetry anthologies and college courses. According to Roger Scruton:

> Campbell wrote vigorous rhyming pentameters, into which he instilled the most prodigious array of images and the most intoxicating draft of life of any poet of the twentieth century. … He was also a swashbuckling adventurer and a dreamer of dreams. And his life and writings contain so many lessons about the British experience in the twentieth century that it is worth revisiting them.

I once wrote an account for *Isis* about how, on one occasion when he was in London in the 1930s, the South African poet Roy

Campbell, known colloquially as the roaring boy, froze the fashionable poet Stephen Spender into silence by loudly throwing open the double doors at the end of the hall in London in which he was reading his poetry.

Health

As I have already mentioned, I lost all hearing in my right ear at the age of nine as a complication of mumps. However, my left ear compensated and I was able to hear the high-pitched calls of bats well into my twenties.

At one point glaucoma endangered my optic nerve, but that was treated under a local anaesthetic. When the South African specialist checked me three months later, however, he popped his head out from a battery of lenses and said, 'you could have gone blind!' I wear glasses for driving and the computer, but can read easily without glasses. In fact, I can even see the features of people walking on the other side of the Thames.

Diagnosis of prostate cancer was a blow for me a couple of decades ago; the operation went well and there have been no secondaries, although I have interrupted nights. I also suffered from a heart arrhythmia, which an electric shock cleared up. Apparently, it often reverts, but fortunately not yet in my case.

Memory loss, both short term and long term, has been a problem. I apparently suffered badly a couple of winters ago, which fortunately I do not remember. This memoir has been a great exercise in bringing back my memory. People remark on how much detail comes back to me, but it is often in the middle of the night.

I have been fortunate with my teeth. On 8 April 2025, Dr Per Dahlmann passed me for another six months while talking about his native Malmö in Sweden, which is near the great bridge to and from Denmark. My neighbour Karin also comes from Malmö.

My great affliction has been a tendency to lose my temper, especially with officials. Clare got me to see the doctor who told me to get a book on anger management, which now looks like a hedgehog because it is so loaded with Post-its. Tamsin has always feared that I might have an outburst. Fortunately, I have never used physical violence. I did on one occasion shout at my Ugandan carer when I felt in the Covid crisis that I should not go to the Radcliffe Hospital without an appointment and that I could wait until the next week when I was already booked in. Afterwards, I always regret that I have lost my temper.

Crude Cruiser cut adrift

For ten weeks from June to August 2025, an unpleasant cabin cruiser was abandoned on the opposite bank. For nights at the end of July it was invaded by rowdy youth and at last the police came to arrest them. The police raid was great entertainment for us and our neighbours safely on our bank. A couple of days later John Ashman quietly cut the blue plastic mooring rope and let the ugly craft drift off down to Folly Bridge and beyond.

Covid will come back year after year

In 2020 an Oxford pharmaceutical company developed a vaccine against Covid, which it tested on Salisbury Plain. The new coronavirus is related to the common cold. Colds are still with us and influenza is now accepted as a yearly epidemic. So probably Covid will be the new virus that will come back each winter.

Handel's Messiah at the Sheldonian

On 12 December 2024, I bought two of the most expensive seats available, because they were accessible for wheelchairs. Rose and I realised we needed to get there early by taxi. We were first in the queue so had to wait outside in the cold until the doors opened at 6.30. Round the corner, out of the wind, there was a beautiful view of the five perpendicular windows of the Divinity School. We were placed in the front row right in the centre behind the conductor with nothing between us and the four soloists. I have never before been in such a perfect position for a concert. We were looking up at the trumpets when they were blasting 'the last trumpet' in the third part. We were feeling the deep throb of the double base and cello. One can see why it is the most popular piece of English music. The Huddersfield Choral Society's performance was renowned. In my snobbish Oxford way, I used to look down on it, especially when compared with Bach. The choir was from Queen's, which was Clare's brother Chris's college, and where, as a scholar, he had a wonderful room overlooking the High Street. After the performance, Rose rolled me in my wheelchair right past the Radcliffe Camera, but we could not stop a taxi in the High Street, so she wheeled me speedily down past the great gates of Christ Church and all the way home.

Oxford Atlas

For Christmas 2024, John had arranged for everybody to club together to get me the latest *Oxford Atlas of the World*. It was a really wonderful present and it includes satellite images from around the world. Atlases had always been important to me ever since I was given the first Oxford Atlas for my fifteenth birthday in 1951.

Tirzah Garwood at the Dulwich Picture Gallery

On 1 March 2025, John drove Rose and me through endless west and south London streets before getting to the Dulwich

Picture Gallery in Camberwell. Having become familiar with Tirzah Garwood's work through the wonderful Fleece Press books, I found the exhibition a bit disappointing. Anyhow, it was informative to see her paintings in the context of the tragedies in her life. It was an inspiration to pair her with her first husband Eric Ravilious from the Eastbourne School of Art who had been killed in a flying boat off Iceland during the war. Ravilious's paintings were twice as big and right for exhibition and I enjoyed them. It was so right that Hal should have lent the painting of the Snowmen at Hedingham, which Henry Swanzy had given to Ralph and Stella, to the gallery. It was splendid to see a portrait of Henry Swanzy, producer of the 'Caribbean Voices' series on the BBC Colonial Service.

The Elams and the Curreys

As we have established, Nick Elam and Andrew Currey were teenage friends, Nick's father Jack was headmaster of the Colchester Royal Grammar School (CRGS) and my father, the poet R. N. Currey, was on his staff. Jack Elam hated the ordeal of working out the school timetable, but always ensured my father had all his free periods on Wednesdays so he could get to London to see publishers, record BBC broadcasts and visit the writers' pubs in Fitzrovia.

Nick was often at our house when my parents entertained writers from Africa and the Caribbean. He told me that he first learnt about sculpture through my parents' copies of the Phaidon library of art books and in particular one on Donatello. This was to lead to his great patronage of sculptors and painters when he was the British ambassador in Luxembourg.

Nick Elam's memorial in St Giles Church in Camberwell was beautifully appropriate. Madrigals were sung by the a cappella group that Nicholas had formed in the embassy in Luxemburg. At drinks afterwards, his Dutch widow and I had a rewarding talk together. They had met when she was at the French embassy in Cape Town and, as with Clare and myself, had the good fortune of being able to enjoy their first year of marriage in the Cape. An Elam cousin told me how she remembered Andrew and Nick staying with them in Taunton when cycling to Timberscombe. Vicky Unwin and I were also able on that occasion to have a long talk together.

It took John three hours to drive Rose's Ford back to Oxford from Camberwell. When we reached the filling station the gauge arrow was pointing at the bottom of empty, but Rose was confident the car would make it. I nervously had John having to walk off into the night. We also filled up with pizza to eat when we got back after a wonderful day.

Simon Gikandi and All Souls College

Simon Gikandi is a professor at Princeton whom Henry Chakava discovered in Nairobi and found that, even as a student, he made imaginative editorial contributions to the publishing of new titles and new authors in the African Writers Series. On 12 March 2025, he was invited to give a lecture at All Souls, one of the most prestigious of the Oxford colleges. It was to take place in the Codrington Library, which had been built in the seventeenth century with money donated by a slave owner from Barbados. Consequently, he based his lecture on 'The antimonies of Atlantic slavery', in other words the paradox of maintaining that the moral law is not binding on Christians. Here he was speaking as a former colonial subject reflecting on the ironies of his giving a lecture there. He acknowledged me publicly as a former colleague and publisher.

Bats fly through my life

The evening after the Gikandi lecture at All Souls, I was sitting with Karin and Joe in their garden by the river in the dusk and the sky was alive with bats. Their elegant cat was driven mad and scampered up the trellis and ran maddened back and forth on the roof. When we were undergraduates Clare and friends and I had been sitting in the dark outside her thatched cottage Paddocks Wells and I turned out to be the only person who could hear the bat sounds. I could still hear the high frequencies I had been able to capture when I went deaf in my left ear at the age of nine. Later, sitting outside the Mill at Walkern, I could hear them as the house martins flew round among them – 'the temple haunting martlets' as they are called in *Macbeth*. I asked a woodman to trim off a broken branch in the ash by the summerhouse. After climbing the tree he told me that he could not legally touch it because it had become a bats' dormitory.

Jenn Ogilvie clears the last fence

On 21 March 2025, the spring equinox, Hal wheeled me into Jenn Ogilvie's funeral at St Michael and All Angels' church in Summertown. Jenn Ogilvie, Gilia Whitehead and Clare Currey had been a trio at St Anne's College, and Jenn eventually came to live next door to us in Thames Street. She had grown up in Argentina and Canada. Her looks were plain but when she had only just graduated, she married Robert Ogilvie, the renowned and handsome classics don at Balliol College and son of Lady Ogilvie, the then principal of St Anne's. They had a farmhouse called Erracht within sight of Ben Nevis. Its garage had a remarkable wall of empty wine bottles and Robert Ogilvie, who by then had become a professor at the University of St Andrews, died. Jenn asked Clare to let her know when a house came up for sale in Thames Street and she became our neighbour until she went into a nursing home. When Hal and Tamsin went to tell her in 2016 that Clare had died, she said, 'Well done Clare, you've cleared the last fence.'

The Grand National

On 5 April 2025, Tamsin came to Thames Street en route by train via Oxford, Leamington Spa and Birmingham to Liverpool where her daughter Hattie had invited her for the renowned steeplechase race. Like the Oxford and Cambridge Boat Race, this has become a national event. In Beverley Road, Ralph and Stella had had a Mrs Becher as a neighbour and she had belonged to the family after which Becher's Brook was named. It acquired its name after the very first Grand National in the mid-nineteenth century when a Captain Martin Becher fell off his horse at the first fence, but sensibly lay in a brook until all the horses had passed by.

Down at the Worcester country club

On 2 April 2025 I went to an evening meeting of the Historical Society at Worcester College and I was wheeled to an elegant modern hall called the Sultan Nazrin Shah Centre. It was a bright evening and we sat down by an ornamental pond. Another attender said she had been shown an aerial photograph and on asking what the large green area was, was told that it was the Worcester grounds and lake. I was interviewed for a scholarship to go to Worcester and told that, as I had already been accepted as a commoner at Wadham, I should go there. I really would have rather liked to go to Worcester.

Conclusion

I was offered two jobs after completing my Oxford history degree and felt torn between book publishing and magazine journalism. I was especially interested in typography, but am glad that I chose the publishing route.

When Oxford University Press sent me to South Africa in 1969, I felt fortunate to be entering publishing just as decolonisation was spreading throughout Africa. However, it would take another thirty years before apartheid was formally ended. The more I became frustrated by the lack of progress in South Africa the more cheered I was by what was happening in the rest of Africa.

Randolph Vigne started the *New African* to cover 'Africa in general and South Africa in particular'.

We had now made young Africans feel that there was hope that they might be published in London. In fact, my own book, *Africa Writes Back*, records the contribution of the African Writers Series to the launch of African literature. With titles such as *Africa Works* and *Congo–Paris*, African Issues aimed to become the Pelicans or Penguins of Africa. Also, with the help of Ian Randle in Jamaica, we had managed to start a Caribbean Writers Series.

I had got California University Press to bid with me for the *UNESCO General History of Africa* in eight volumes. We prepared volume 8 for press, which was edited by Ali A. Mazrui under the title *Africa since 1935*. President Gaddafi of Libya paid for the entire series. UNESCO took its Portuguese, French, English, Chinese and Arabic publishers to celebrate at Gaddafi's camp in the Libyan desert near Sirte.

Hannah and Ella Currey at Sant Antonio, Tivoli May 1999

And finally, to top it all, we almost always managed to get our titles co-published in all three of the continents of America, Europe and Africa. The James Currey Collection at St Cross College in Oxford contains all 1200 of our published titles. I started this book to show my granddaughters just how valuable Clare's partnership with me had been to our success at building the most outstanding list of books on Africa.

Index

A

A Level exam, 26, 33, 41, 127
Aase, Jan, 108
Abbotsholme, 128
Abdalla, Abdilatif, 152
Abrahams, Ibraham, 71, 76, 87
Accra, 92
Achebe, 151
Achebe, Chinua, 136–8, 140–1, 148–50, 151, 158, 162, 184
Achebe, Christie, 141
Adderley Street, 72, 80
Addis Ababa, 135, 144
Africa, 1, 27, 50–1, 60, 67, 72–3, 85, 90, 92, 99, 106–7, 116–17, 126, 135, 137, 139, 141, 147, 156, 159–60, 163, 166, 169, 177, 181, 185, 187, 191, 194, 199, 208, 211, 212
Africa Bureau, 72
Africa Centre, 146, 180
African National Congress (ANC), 53, 82, 103
African Resistance Movement (ARM), 53, 105
African Service, BBC, 154
African Studies Association (ASA), 182, 184
African Universities Press, 187
African Writers Series, 1, 116, 136, 137–40, 142, 147–8, 150–1, 155–8, 160, 164–9, 173, 179, 181, 184–5, 209, 212
Afrikaners, 48, 54, 57, 111
Albemarle Ladies Club, 117, 135

Aldeburgh, 1
Alexandria, 162
Alison, Clive, 176
Alitalia, 111–12
All Blacks, NZ, 153
All Souls College, Oxford, 209
Allies, 16
Amadi, Elechi, 150
Amen House, OUP, 46–7, 112, 117
America, 36, 47, 77, 85, 90, 117, 136, 146, 177, 181, 184, 212; American, 5, 18, 29, 31, 41, 61, 64, 69, 74, 145, 160, 173, 178, 182, 184, 191, 194; Americans, 42, 180, 182; *see also* United States
American University in Cairo Press, 162
Amherst College, 74
Amin, Idi, 188
Amsterdam, 41
André Deutsch, 186
Anglo American, 74
Angola, 78
anti-colonial resistance, 193
Antwerp, 41
Apapa, 169
apartheid, 47, 49, 51–2, 56–7, 61, 82, 88, 198, 211
Arab Authors, 173; Arab Authors Series, 166, 169
Arabic, 162–3, 166, 212
Arabs, 107
Aregay, Merid Wolde, 144
Argentina, 210; Argentinians, 125
Armah, Ayi Kwei, 140, 157
Arnhem, 16

213

INDEX

Ashanti, 184
Ashman, John, ix, 207–9
Astor, David, 60
Athenaeum Club, 141, 178
Athens, 96
Atlantic Ocean, 51, 72, 115, 131, 209
atom bomb, 18, 194
August, Collingwood, 90
Auschwitz, 14
Austen, Jane, 105
Australia, 47, 123, 199; Australian, 57, 77, 199; Australians, 10
Austria, 15
Automobile Association (AA), 194
Auvergne, 41

B

Bach, Johann Sebastian, 65, 195, 207
Badby Road, Daventry, 10, 12
Baldwin, Alan, 86
Balkema, A. A., 58
Balkerne Gate, Colchester, 3
Balliol College, Oxford, 37, 175, 210
Baltic, 41
Banda, President, Malawi, 80, 134
Bangalore, 201
Bank of England, 60
Bannister, Dr Roger, 30
bantustan, 64, 113; bantustans, 100
Baobab Press, 185
Barbados, 209
Barclays Bank, 179
Bard College, NY, 184
Barnard, Christiaan, 152
Barnes, Mr, 20
Barros, Rose, ix, 206, 208
Basotho, 90; Basutoland (Lesotho), 60, 67, 90
Bath, xiii, xiv, 8, 20, 26, 28–30, 195–6, 201; Bath Abbey, 197; Bath Spa, 28

Batt, Algy, 28
Battle of Britain, 4, 6
Bauhaus, 45
Bay Beach, 131
Bay House, Tresco, 130–1
BBC, xiv, 9, 35, 44, 56, 160, 163, 182, 199, 208; Colonial Service, 167, 208; Empire Service, 10; Hausa Service, 117
Beal, Tony, 158
Becher, Captain Martin, 211
Bechuanaland (Botswana), 60, 68, 76, 90, 108
Bedales School, 127
Bedford Square, Heinemann, 177
Beirut, 162–3
Beit Bridge, South Africa–Rhodesia, 103, 105
Belgian Congo, 90; see also Congo
Belgium, 3, 9, 16, 21, 53
Bell, Kate (maternal grandparents' maid), 6, 12, 14
Belsen, 33
Ben Nevis, 210
Berlin Festival, 1977, 155
Berlin Wall, 53
Beti, Mongo, 139, 149, 158, 164
Beverley Road, Colchester, 1, 3–4, 17–18, 23, 27, 114, 194, 211
Biafran, 136, 140–1, 150
Biafran War, 159
Bickmore, David, OUP, 46
Bida, Nigeria, 140
Bigsby, Jack, builder, 133–4
Bijl, Val, 64
Birmingham, 50, 172, 210
Bishop, Adrian, 27, 33
Bishop Rock, Scilly, 195
Black Hall, St Johns, 38
Black Sash, South Africa, 67, 81, 98
Black, Kitty, literary agent, 57
Bloomsbury set, 133
Blunt, David, Heinemann, 171, 174
Blythe, Ronald, 1, 24, 155–6
Bochum, South Africa, 104

214

INDEX

Bodleian, Oxford, 36, 39–41
Boer War memorial, Cape Town, 81
Bombay, 19, 194
Bosnia, 197
Botley Road, JCP Office, 116
Botswana, 60, 155–6; see also under Bechuanaland
Bowater, Bill, 108
Bowra, Sir Maurice, 34–5, 37–8, 63
Bragg, Melvyn, 44
Brand, Dollar, 59
Bristol, xiv, 14, 28, 35, 101
Bristol Hotel, Lagos, 140
Britain, 6, 15, 19, 25, 49, 57, 68, 85, 92, 96, 101, 106, 121, 155, 177, 182
Britanno-Roman ramparts, 3
British Council, 37–8
British High Commission Territories, 90
British Museum, 187
British Tyre and Rubber Company (BTR), 171, 185
British Union of Fascists, 204
Brokkes Nek, 69
Bromberger, Norman, 108
Brookes University, Oxford, 113
Brown, Sir John, 46, 112, 135
Brown, Leonard, 122
Brown's Hotel, 177
Bruges, 3
Brunner, Hugo, 47, 135, 180
Brunner Mond & Company, 48
Brutalist architects, 37
Brutus, Dennis, 149, 152
Bryanston School, 30
Bryher, 131–2
Bunga, Transkei, 83, 100
Buntingford, 124, 127, 201
Bureau of State Security (BOSS), South Africa, 105–6
Burnham scale, schoolmasters, 40
Busby, Margaret, 176

Butler, Penny, 168
Butler, R. A., 17, 35

C

Cacanas, George, 3, 38, 197
Cacanas, Joanna (née Roberts), ix 195–7, 201–2
Cacanas, Rachel, 195
Cairo, 96, 161–2, 166
Caledon Square, 66–7
Caledonian Road, 133, 181, 186
California, 182, 199
California University Press, 212
Camberwell, 208–9
Cambourne, 120
Cambridge, 26, 28, 31, 33, 93, 107, 114–15, 117, 120, 124, 135, 165, 168, 187, 190, 195, 211
Cambridge, University of, 27, 93, 127; Department of Aerial Photography, 115
Cambridge University Press, 175, 181–2, 190
Cameroun, 92, 164
Campbell, Catherine, 190
Campbell, Roy, 43, 204–5
Camps Bay (Cape Town), 72
Canada, 108, 110, 185, 210; Canadian, 182; Canadians, 10, 111
Cannes, 42
Cannon, Freddie, 61, 72, 75, 111
Cape Town, 9, 25, 47, 50–1, 53–4, 58–61, 64, 66–9, 71–2, 77–8, 80, 85, 89–90, 93, 96, 98, 100–1, 106–8, 111, 113, 115, 152, 175, 190, 198, 208; Book Fair, 185
Caribbean, 27, 136, 148, 167, 173–4, 176, 181, 208
Caribbean Voices, 34, 167, 208
Caribbean Writers Series, 148, 167, 169, 173, 212
Carlisle, 40
Carolina, Transvaal, 71
Carrington, Lord, 125

215

INDEX

Carson, Rachel, 41
Casablanca, 35
Castle Hedingham, 167
Caterick Camp, 35
Cato Manor, 89
Cecil, Lord David, xiii
Censorship Act, South Africa, 83
Centlivres, Lord Chief Justice, 81
Central Hotel, Mbabane, 87
Central Intelligency Agency (CIA), 85, 137
Central School of Arts and Crafts, 49, 58
Chakava, Henry, 142, 160, 209
Chamberlin, Joseph, 199
Chartres, 42
Chatto & Windus, 48, 180
Chavasse, Gabrielle, 93
Chelsea, 49, 159
Cheltenham, 36
Chester, Philip, 47, 113, 135
Chesterman, Jimmy, 127, 172–3
Chesterman, Shirley, 127, 172
Chesterman family, 172
China, 199; Chinese, 212
cholera, 199
Christ Church, Oxford, 36, 207
Chuck, Neville, 125
Church of England, 28
Churchill Hospital, Oxford, 190
Ciskei, 113
Citizens Advice Bureau, 178
City of Bath School, 30
civil war, 13, 40, 136
Claremont Hall, 98
Clarendon Press, 46–7, 181
Clark, J. P., 116
Clarke, Philip, 199
Clerkenwell, 154
Clevedon, 14, 18
Clifden, 115
Clifton, 51
Clifton House, 59, 108
Cloete, Andreas, 78
Clough, Juliet, 124
Clouts, Sidney, 54
Clyde, River, 25
Codrington Library, All Souls, Oxford, 209
Cohen, Bernard, artist, 6
Colchester, 1, 3–5, 17, 21, 34, 36, 39, 42, 49, 114, 116, 167, 208
Colchester Castle, 3
Colchester Literary Society, 24
Colchester Repertory Theatre, xiv
Colchester Royal Grammar School (CRGS), x, xiv, 1, 8, 17, 25–9, 34, 112, 208
Collings, Rex, 113, 116–17, 135, 146; Rex Collings Ltd, 146
Collins Fontana, 159
Colorado beetle, 10
Commonwealth, 15, 47, 57, 81, 185
Commonwealth Prime Ministers' Conference, 1961, 81
Communist Party, 53
communists, 53, 83
Company's Garden, 58
comprehensive schools, 26, 128
Conakry, 92
Conference of African Writers of English Expression, Makerere, 85
Congo, 101, 112, 191, 212; see also under Belgian Congo
Congress for Cultural Freedom, 85, 137, 139
Conrad, Joseph, 105, 119
conscientious objector, 39
Constable, John, 48
Constantia, 73
Contact, 60, 63–4, 71–2, 74, 82–3, 87, 90
Cook, Hammond and Kell Ltd, 46
Cookham, 37
Co-operative Bank, 201
Copenhagen, 102, 188
Copford, 167
Cornwall, xiii, 130–1
coronavirus, 199, 203–4, 207; see also Covid

INDEX

Corpus Christi College, Oxford, 68
Cottered, 93, 106, 115, 121, 124–6
Covid, 195, 201–2, 206; *see also* coronavirus
Cranks, 126
Craven, John, 145
Crawford, Archie, 40
Crewdson, Ingrid, 176, 178
Cromwell, Oliver, 40, 129, 132
Crouch Street, 23
Crowder, Michael, 169
Crummey, Donald, 146
Culdrose, 131
Culver, Aunt Joan, 3–4, 25, 36, 38, 114
Culver, Harold, 114
Cumbria, xii
Cunningham, Joe, 203, 209
Curling, Jonathan, 34
Currey, Andrew (brother), xv, 4–8, 10–18, 20, 22, 24–8, 31, 34, 208–9
Currey, Aunt Sally, 6
Currey, Clare (née Wilson), 1, 3, 26–7, 30, 38–40, 42, 48–9, 54, 70, 92–3, 95–6, 98–9, 101, 103, 106–8, 110–12, 114–18, 120–1, 123–9, 131–5, 144–5, 153, 172–3, 178, 180–1, 184–5, 190, 194–5, 197–8, 200, 202, 204–5, 207, 208–10, 212
Currey, Edith (née Vinnicombe, paternal grandmother), xiii, 7, 41, 54, 121
Currey, Ella (granddaughter), 1
Currey, Hal (son), 26, 116–18, 120–2, 124–5, 127, 129, 132–3, 145, 167, 190, 201, 204, 208, 210
Currey, Hannah (granddaughter), 1
Currey, Ian (Uncle), 10
Currey, John (paternal grandfather), xii, xiii, 7, 56, 167
Currey, Ralph N. (father), x, xiii–xv, 1, 3–7, 9, 17–19, 21–4, 26–8, 34–7, 40, 43–4, 47, 50, 54, 56, 62, 65, 112–14, 116, 167–8, 184, 204, 208–9, 211
Currey, Ronald H. M., xiii
Currey, Sophie (née Cohen, daughter-in-law), 6
Currey, Stella (mother), xiii–xv, 1, 3–8, 12–14, 16–17, 19–20, 22–4, 26, 27–9, 36–7, 50, 54, 56–7, 95, 112, 114, 167, 208, 211
Currey, Tamsin (daughter), 26, 120, 122–5, 128–9, 132, 145, 173, 188, 190, 195–6, 201, 204, 206, 210
Currey, Tom (father's brother), 5
Currey, Tom (no relation), xiii
Currey family, 6, 41
Curtis Brown, 29
Cutting Hill Farm, 172
Czech, 168; Czechoslovakia, 6, 14

D

Daba, Tsefaye, 135
Dahlmann, Dr, 205
Dakar, 92, 139, 163
Dakin, Mr, 32
Danida, 188
Dar es Salaam, 175
Daventry, 6, 8, 10, 15, 17–18
Davidson, Basil, 194
Davis, Caroline, 113
de Grunne, Dominic, 41
de Waal, Alex, 191
de Waal, Edmund, 28
De Waal Drive, Cape Town, 91
de Water, Charles, 57, 65
decolonisation, 49, 60, 137, 151, 211
Dedham, 48
Defiance Campaign, 66
Delius, Anthony, 54, 57, 82, 85–6
Denmark, 101, 188, 205; Danish, 102, 188
Derbyshire, 128
Deutsch, André, 44, 148
Deutsche Welle, 61, 172
Devonshire, xiii

INDEX

Dickens, Charles, 105
Die Burger, 54, 65, 73–4
Dinky Toys, 22
Disney, Walt, 9
District Six, Cape Town, 59, 64, 152
Divinity School, Oxford, 207
Dollar Brand, 59
Donatello, 27, 208
Donne, John, 58–9
Douala, 92
Double Storey Books, Cape Town, 190
Douglas-Home, Sir Alec, 70
Drum, 77–8
Dublin, 115
Duerden, Dennis, 117
Dulwich Picture Gallery, 167, 207–8
Duncan, Cynthia (née Ashley Cooper), 51, 60
Duncan, Patrick, 50–1, 60–1, 64, 67, 75–6, 82–3, 87–8, 90, 133
Duncan Docks, 61
Dunkery Beacon, 21
Dunster, 21
Durban, 68, 89, 113
Dusseldorf, 93, 106
Dutch, 27, 51, 54, 56, 78, 86, 208
Dutch East India Company, 51, 78
Dutch Reformed Church, 54, 56
Dyson, Mary, 117, 135

E

Ealing Studios, 24
East Africa, 151, 168; East African, 35, 139, 150
East African Examinations Council (EAEC), 139, 158
East African Navy, 35
East African Publishing House (EAPH), 160, 187
East Herts Council, 124
East London, 100
Eastbourne School of Art, 208
Eastern Cape, 64, 66

Echeruo, Michael, 161
Economist Building, 37
Edinburgh, 115, 171
Edmark, 43
Education Act, 17, 35, 88
Egypt, 161, 166; Egyptians, 161
Ekwensi, Cyprian, 138, 140, 149, 158–9
Elam, Helen, 27
Elam, Jack, 27
Elam, Nicholas (Nick), 27, 112, 208–9
eleven-plus exam, 17, 25–6, 128
Eliot, George, 105
Eliot, T. S., xiv, 139
Elizabeth I, Queen, xiv, 17, 47
Elliot, Zoe (née Cacanas), 195–6
Ely House, 117, 135
Emecheta, Buchi, 149, 159
England, 5–6, 9, 21, 26, 37, 41, 43, 61, 70, 114, 138, 159–60, 185, 187
Entoto Mariam, Addis Ababa, 144
Ermelo, 56, 71
Erracht, 210
Essex, 22, 36
Ethiopia, 144–6, 191
Ethiopian Airlines, 145
Europe, 6, 15, 18, 20, 24, 38, 159, 166, 181, 212
Everyman Classics, 180
Exmoor, 20

F

Fagunwa, Chief, 140
Falkland Islands, 125
Far East, 25, 133
Farringdon, 121
Fellows Garden, Wadham, 40
Finnegan, Ruth, 193
Finnish, 188
First World War, xiv, 39
Fisher, Robson, 30, 33
Fitzrovia, 208
Fleece Press, 208

INDEX

Fleet Air Arm, 131
Flemish National Theatre, 53
Florence, 42
Flynn, Campbell, 134
Folly Bridge, 116, 199, 206
Fone, Miss, 44
Fonthill Road, 30
Ford, Malcolm, 8
Foreign Office, 27, 112, 125
Foreshore, Cape Town, 61
Fourah Bay College, 139
Fowles, John, 162
France, 5, 9, 41, 92; French, 9, 18, 20, 24, 31, 33, 38, 41–2, 137, 139, 158, 163–4, 177, 193, 208, 212
Frankfurt Book Fair, 172
Fransen, Hans, 65
Freetown, 25
Fremer, Karin, 199, 205, 209
French, *see under* France
Freudian, 40
Friends Meeting House, 93, 128
Fugard, Athol, 77

G

Gaddafi, Muammar, 193, 212
Gale, Richard, 171, 175
Gallman, John, 182
Gardner, John, 30
Garlicks, 61
Garnett, Angelica, 133
Garwood, Tirzah, 167, 207–8
GCSE, 21, 30, 33
Geneva, 41, 64, 200
German World Service, 172
Germany, 4, 15–17, 36, 48, 101, 144; German, 6, 16, 20, 37, 86, 101, 129, 155; Germans, 6, 14–15
Ghana, 49, 92, 137, 140, 184; Ghanaian, 140, 157
Gibraltar, 124
Gibson, Rufus, 34, 66
Gikandi, Simon, 148, 209
Gikuyu, 151

Gittings, Robert, 48
Glasgow College of Art, 121
Glenthorne, 129
global warming, 41
Godwin, David, 179
Gog Magog Hills, 93
Gold Coast, 167
Goldreich, Arthur, 76
Gollancz, 155
Gombrich, Ernst, 49
Gordimer, Nadine, 76, 147
Gourock, 25
Gracey (bookseller), 113
Grahamstown, 64, 89
grammar schools, 26
Grand Parade, Bath, 80–1
Grant, Duncan, 133
Graschenkov, Chairman, WHO, 200
Grasmere, 129
Great Russell Street, 187
Greef, Officer, South African Special Branch, 71
Greek, 27; General, 197
Green Howards, 28
Grieve, Muire, 98
Griggs, Mr, 24
Groote Schuur Hospital, Cape Town, 152
Group Areas Act, 59, 77
Guardian Fiction Prize, 1979, 155
Gugler, Josef, 193
Guinea, 92
Gulf, 166, 182; Gulf states, 166
Gunton, Mr, 23
Gurnah, Abdulrazak, 147
Gutenberg, Johannes, 190

H

Haifa, 19
Hall, A. F., 3
Hamer, Andrew, 21
Hamish Hamilton, 61
Hampshire, 127
Hanbury-Tenison, Marika, 130

INDEX

Hanbury-Tenison, Robin, 129, 204
Hancock, Matt, 203
Handley Page, 9
Hanover Street, 59
Hansen, Holger Bernt, 188
Harley Street, 39, 92
Harris, John, 70
Harvard, 76
Head, Bessie, 149, 155–6
Hearsums, 23
Heathrow, 96, 112, 141, 155
Heinemann, 116, 135, 137–8, 140, 142–3, 148, 151–2, 154, 159–60, 166, 168–9, 171–7, 179, 181–2, 184–5, 191
Heinemann Educational Books, 116, 159, 165, 170, 174, 178–9
Heinemann Group, 171
Heinemann Nigeria, 140
Helm, Richard, 177
Helsinki, 190, 202
Helsinki University, 188
Hendon, 90
Henley, 135
Henry VIII, King, xiv, 17
Henshilwood, Norah, 74, 98
Hermanus, 78
Hertford, 128
Hertfordshire, 115–17, 121, 124–5, 127–8, 182, 194
Hertfordshire, North, 120
Heusler, Dagmar, 155
Higgs, Cecil, 74
High Commission Territories, 68, 76
High Street, Oxford, 43
Higo, Aigboje (Aig), 139–40, 142–3, 146, 150
Hill, Alan, 136–8, 140–1, 144, 169, 175, 177
Hiroshima, 194
Historical Society, 211
Hitchin, 179
Hitler, Adolf, 5–6
HIV/AIDS, 190
Hjul, Peter, 109

Holburne Museum, 195
Holmes, Sally, 106
Holmes, Tim, 50, 64, 71–2, 74, 81, 83, 87, 106
Holmfirth, 7
Home, Lord; *see* Douglas-Home, Sir Alec, 70
Home Service, BBC, 56
Hong Kong, 48
Hospital for Tropical Diseases, 119
Hotel Cosmopolitan, Cairo, 96
Hôtel de France, Conakry, 92
HSBC, 201
Huddersfield, 7–8
Huddersfield Choral Society, 207
Hughes-Davis, Jimmy, 47
Hugh-Jones, Stephen, 43, 200
Hulton Press, 45
Hunt, John, 137
Hurst, Christopher, 180, 186
Hutchinson, Val, 68, 73, 159
Huxley, Elspeth, 156

I

Ibadan, 85, 92, 116, 140, 142, 147, 170
Ibrahim, Abdullah, 59
Iceland, 167, 208
ICI, 48
Ifeld, 20
Iffley Road, Oxford, 30
Igbo, Nigeria, 141
Iliffe, John, 190
Imperial Chemical Industries (ICI), 48
imperialism, 53, 193
India, 9, 17, 19–20, 47, 194; Indians, 10
Indian Army, 47
Indian Civil Service, 112
Indian Ocean, 51
Indiana University Press, 182

INDEX

influenza, 207
Ipswich, 4, 25
Isis, 39, 43–5, 58, 198, 200
Isle of Man, 130
Isles of Scilly, 195
Islington, 115, 176–8, 186
Italy, 41–2, 45, 170; Italian, 24–5, 42, 45, 144, 177; Italians, 14, 197

J

J. M. Dent & Sons, 180
Jamaica, 167, 173, 212
James Currey Collection, St Cross, 212
James Currey Publishers, 76, 115, 127, 168, 172, 175–6, 181, 184, 187
James Fort Prison, 152
James, P. D., 28
James, Wendy, 115, 191
Jam Smuts Airport, South Africa, 112
Japan, 17–18, 25; Japanese, 194
Jenkins, Arthur, 68
Jericho, Ibadan, 169
Jew, 10, 143; Jewish, 14, 59, 182; Jews, 15
Johannesburg, 50, 61, 70, 74, 77, 89, 103, 108, 111–12, 152
John Murray, 61, 171
John Radcliffe Hospital, Oxford, 68, 195, 206
Johnson, Douglas, 115, 191
Johnson, Jonathan, 18, 20
Johnson, Judith, 18
Johnson, Leonie, 18, 36
Johnson-Davies, Denys, 162–3, 166
Jonathan Cape, xv, 61, 179, 203
Juta, 190

K

Kamiti Maximum Security Prison, 151
Kampala, 85
Kamusinga, 143
Kanafani, Ghassan, 166
Kandahar, 197
Karoo, 83, 100
Kaunda, Kenneth, 138, 144, 169
Keeler, Christine, 105
Kelly, Sonya, 199, 201
Kelvin Grove Club, 83
Kennedy, John F., 70, 74
Kent, 9
Kenya, 138, 144, 155, 158, 161, 202; Kenyan, 49, 151, 161
Kenyatta, Jomo, 151
Kgosana, Philip, 66–7
Khama, Tshekedi, 156
Khartoum, 50, 162
Kindertransport, 6, 14
King, Martin Luther, 64
King's Cross, 133, 187
Kingsthorpe, Daventry, 8
Kingswood School, x, xiii–xiv, 20, 26–31, 33, 35–6, 133, 167
King William's Town, 113
Kinshasa, 101, 112
Kirwood, Margaret, 65
Kirwood, Mary, 64–5, 72
Kivukoni College, 175
Klerksdorp, 88
Kloof Nek Road, Cape Town, 96
Knaplock Farm, Exmoor, 20
Knokke, 16
Kok, Dr, 60
Kokstad, 69
Kommetjie, 74, 98
Koomson, Abraham, 157
Korea, 32; Korean War, 32
Kruschev, Nikita, 105
Kunene, Mazisi, 157

L

La Guma, Alex, 82, 149, 152
Labour Party, 96
Lagos, 92, 137, 140, 146, 169
Lake District, 129, 133

INDEX

Lalibela, 145
Lamb, Lynton, 47
Langa, 63, 66
Langford, Alistair, 127
Lasdun, Denys, 28
Latin, 27, 33, 38, 96, 166
Latin America, 38
Laughton, Charles, 119
Lausanne, 26, 38
Lawler, Ray, 77
Lawrence of Arabia, 24
Le Puy-en-Velay, 41, 42
League of Nations, 57–8
Leamington Spa, 12, 210
Leeds, University of, 116
Lee-Warden, Len, 86
Leftwich, Adrian, 108
Legum, Colin, 86
Leribe, 90
Lesotho, 60, 67
Lessing, Doris, 147, 157
Letchworth/Letchworth Garden City, 120, 126, 128, 180
Lewin, Hugh, 100
Leys, Colin, 175
Liberal, 52, 60–1, 64, 68, 88, 99
Liberal Party, 52, 61, 64, 68–70, 73, 77–8, 80–1, 83, 86, 88, 99, 110
Liberator bomber, 19
Libya, 12, 193, 212; Libyans, 193
Lichfield, 134
Lincoln, 37; Lincolnshire, 40
Linder, (Aunt) Iris, 78, 107
Linder, Iver (Uncle), 78
Lindfors, Bernth, 184
Lion's Head, 59, 98
Liverpool, 5, 14, 49, 114, 210
Liverpool Street, 5, 14, 49, 114
London, 3, 5–7, 14–15, 17, 22, 24, 27, 30, 37, 43, 48, 54, 56–7, 60–1, 63, 65, 72, 85–6, 93, 110, 112–13, 115–17, 133, 135–6, 140–2, 145, 148, 159, 162–3, 165–7, 174, 177, 179, 186, 188, 204, 208–9

London and North Eastern Railway (LNER), 24
London College of Printing, 58
Longinus tombstone, 3
Longman, 181, 187
Lonsdale, Sarah, xiv, 29
Louw, Joseph, 59, 64
Luce, Richard, 124–5, 202
Luce, Rose, 124, 202
Lucy Cavendish College, 127
Luftwaffe, 6
Lumumba, Patrice, 101
Lusaka, 106, 144
Luthuli, Chief Albert, 53
Luxembourg, 27, 208
Lynd, Moira, 159

M

McCracken, Gabrielle, 38
MacGibbon, Hamiah, 168
Mackendrick, Alexander, 24
Macleod, Iain, 49
Macmillan, Harold, 49, 57
Macmillan Press, 181
Mâcon, 42
Madrid, 37
Mafeking, xiii, 108
Mafoko, Carl, 103
Mahfouz, Naguib, 161–2
Makerere University, 85, 137–8, 139, 160
Malawi, 80, 105–6; *see also* Nyasaland
Malay, 87; Malayan, 49
Malaya, 34
Malmö, 205
Manchester, 133, 188
Manchester University Press (MUP), 180, 187
Mandela, Nelson, 53, 64, 82
Mandela, Winnie, 103
Marechera, Dambudzo, 153–4, 184
Margery (helper), 145
Markham, Bob, 143
Markham, Susannah, 143

INDEX

Marquard, Leo, 48, 54, 58, 61, 66–7, 72, 75, 88, 107, 113
Marquard, Nell, 48
Marston Moor, Battle of, 31
Martin, Alice, 188, 202
Martin, Hal (mother's brother), 19, 20, 40, 188
Martin, J. P. (maternal grandfather), xiii, xv, 6–7, 11, 13, 15–16, 18, 21, 28, 95, 128, 199
Martin, Jane (great aunt), 5, 21
Martin, John (mother's brother), 12, 16
Martin, Mairie, 188
Martin, Nancy (née Mann, maternal grandmother), xiii, 6, 8, 12
Martin, Norman (great-uncle), 15
Martin family, xiii, 8, 28
Marx, Groucho, 105
Marx, Karl, 105
Maryport, xii
Maseru, 68, 90
Matanzima, Chief, 70, 83
Mau Mau, 49
Maupassant, Guy de, 41
Mauriac, Claude, 163
Mayfair, 136
Mazrui, Ali A., 160, 182, 212
Mbabane, 87
Mbari Club, Ibadan, 116
Meccano, 22
Meetings for Sufferings, Quakers, 128
Meli, Francis, 53
Melluish, Stewart, 47
Memphis, 64
Mendips, 194
Methodist, 6–7, 9, 11, 13, 16, 28, 36, 56, 128
Methodist Church, 167; Methodists, 29, 95
Methuen Publishers, 116, 146
Meyer, Dr Bryan, 7
Meyer, Elspeth, 7–8
Meyer, Jenny, 7

Mgudlandlu, Gladys, 74
Michie, James, 137
Midland Bank, 154
Mid-Western Region, Nigeria, 140
Millar, Anthony, 51, 63, 66, 96
Millar, Joy, 51, 57, 63, 96
Miller, William, 44
Milne, Van, 138
MINDECO, Zambia, 144
MMR vaccine, 17
Mokholo, Jacob, 103
Molteno, Robert, 187, 195
Mombasa, 151, 182
Montreal, 111
Morgan, Sally, 59
Morocco, 41
Morris, James, 48
Moser, Dr, 10
Moser, Matthew, 10, 12, 15
Mosley, Sir Oswald, 204
Mosotho, 68
Mount Currie, 69
Mount Pleasant, Cambridge, 117
Mozambique, 191
Msonthi, John Dunstan, 134
Mulaisho, Dominic, 144
Munali School, Lusaka, 106
Munich, 129; crisis, 121
Museum Road, Oxford, 40
Muslim, 65, 153
Mwangi, Meja, 160

N

Nagasaki, 194
Nairobi, 50, 96, 142–3, 147, 151, 160, 187, 209; University of, 142
Naseby, 13
Nashville, 182
Nasser, Gamal Abdel, 161
Natal, 48, 54, 64–5, 69, 73, 80–1, 86, 88
National Gallery, 43, 57
National Party, 52, 57, 73, 86, 90, 113
National Service, 7, 31, 35

223

INDEX

National Socialist, 20
Nattriss, Miss, 117
Nazi, 20, 33, 59; Nazis, 6, 10, 14, 58, 88
Neal, David, 113, 116, 135
Neasden, OUP, 49
Nel, De Wet, 66, 99
Netherlands, 59
Nettle, Keith, 171, 173
Neville, Jill, 163
New Africa Library, 72
New College, Oxford, 153, 195
New England, 184
New Grimsby Sound (Tresco), Isles of Scilly, 132
New Zealand, 47, 51, 153, 199
Newman, Mr, 122
News Chronicle, 12, 15
Newsom, Sir John, 128
Ngũgĩ wa Thiong'o (James), 138–9, 142, 151, 173
Nichols, Prue (née Hiller), 37
Nicolson, Nigel, 37
Niger, 163
Nigeria, 92, 135, 137–8, 140–1, 143, 146, 150–1, 155, 159, 170, 187; Nigerian, 135, 140, 146, 150–1, 160, 169
Nigerian Civil War, 160
Nigerian Military School, 150
Nile Valley, 96
Nile, River, 163
Nkosi, Lewis, 76, 117
Nkrumah, Kwame, 152, 194
Nobel Prize, 146–7, 150, 161–2
Nobes, Patrick, 27, 127–8
Nododile, Cromwell, 77
Nokia, 190
Nolte, Ferdy and Hélène, 88
Norfolk, 125
Normandy, 16, 28
North Africa, 14, 18
Northern Sotho, 105
Norwegian, 108, 111, 199
Nottingham, John, 187

Nsukka, 141–2
NUSAS, 61
Nyanga, 66, 74
Nyasaland, 60, 106, 134, 175; *see also* Malawi

O

O Level exam, 26–7
O'Hagan, Michael, 134
Official Secrets Act, 25, 44
Ogilvie, Jenn, 210
Ogilvie, Lady, 210
Ogilvie, Robert, 210
Ohio University Press, 182, 185, 190
Ohland, Carl, 101
OK Bazaars, 77
Okigbo, Christopher, 141, 160
Old Bailey, 47, 121
Old India Hand, 135
Olympic Games, 129, 153
Open University, 127, 193
Operation Sea Lion, 5–6
Oppenheimer, Harry, 75
Orpen, Mavis, 74, 98
Ousmane Sembène, 149, 163–4, 193
Ovambo, 78
Oxford, 3, 5, 26, 28, 30–1, 33–6, 40, 43, 47, 49, 64, 88, 93, 111, 114–16, 135, 162, 167, 172, 176–7, 187, 194–7, 199, 207–8, 209–11
Oxford, University of, 26–7, 101, 118, 127, 133
Oxford Brookes University, 113
Oxford International Committee, 37, 39, 128, 133, 200
Oxford Literary Festival, 195
Oxford Preservation Society, 203
Oxford University Centipedes, 30–1
Oxford University Press (OUP), 45–50, 61, 64, 72, 87–90, 92, 96, 105–6, 108, 111–18, 135–6, 146, 162, 168, 175–6, 180–1, 211
Oyono, Ferdinand, 164

INDEX

P

Paarl, 108
Paddington, 28, 131
Paddocks Wells, 117, 120–1, 210
Palestine, 19; Palestinian, 166, 182
Palestine Liberation Organization (PLO), 166
Pan Books, 72, 148, 172
Pan-African Congress (PAC), 53, 66
Pan-African Writers Association, 184
Panama, 167
Paris, 16, 41–2, 58, 64, 85, 137, 163, 191, 193, 212
Parker, Mrs, 120
Parliament Chambers, Cape Town, 60
Parnwell, E. C., 46
Paton, Alan, 52, 61, 73, 88, 98, 100
penguin, 198
Penguin Books, 1, 72, 137, 138, 147–8, 166, 172, 181, 191, 198
Penguin Classics, 155
Penguin Modern Africa Library, 73
Pennines, xii
Penzance, 131
Perkins, Aunt Grace, 14
Persephone Press, xiv, 8, 29
Persia, 147
Petersfield, 127
Pethybridge, Roger, 200
Philby, Kim, 96
Philip, David, xiv, 47, 58, 61, 107, 113, 156
Philip, Dr John, 61
Philip, Marie, 61
Phipson, Mary, 54
Phipson family, 54, 172
Phoenicians, 107
Pierneef, Jacobus Hendrik, 58
Pietermaritzburg, 1, 54, 64–5, 100
Pietersburg, 103
Pilgrim's Rest, xiii
Pledger, Mr, 125
Pluto Press, 187

Plympton, Mrs Calvin, 74
Pogrund, Benjamin, 75
Pondoland, 59, 75
Port Elizabeth, 108
Port Meadow, 38
Porton Down, 203
Portuguese, 107, 212
Prague, 14
Pretoria, 70–1, 75, 103, 105–6, 182
Pretoria High School, 182
Princeton, 148, 209
Prior's Court School, 30
Progressive Party, 53, 80, 82
Public Records Office, 178
punting, 38

Q

Quaker, 93, 98, 101, 128; Quakers, 95
Queen's College, Oxford, 185, 207

R

radar, 9
Radcliffe Camera, 39, 207
Radio South Africa, 70
Rand Club, 152
Randle, Ian, 173, 212
Ranger, Terence, 175
Ransome, Arthur, 17, 20
Ravilious, Eric, 167, 208
Rea, Julian, 181
Reform Club, 178
Regent's Park, 112
Reith Lectures, 160, 182
Rhine, 16
Rhodesia and Nyasaland, University of, 175
Rhodesia, Northern, 105, 144; Southern, 47, 54, 58, 60, 92, 103, 105–6, 144
Rhodes, Cecil John, xiii
Rhodes–Livingstone Institute, 187
Richardson, Paul, 159, 165

INDEX

Rickmansworth, 6
Ridge, Jean, 108, 109
Rio de Janeiro, 25
Rivonia, 93, 202; Rivonia Trial, 103
Robben Island, 77, 152–3
Roberts, Colin, OUP, 46
Roche, Mr, 33
Roeland Street Prison, 72, 152
Roma, 67–8
Roman Catholic, 68
Roman wall, Colchester, 3, 45
Rome, 45, 50, 112; Romans, 3, 21
Roodepoort, xiii
Rosenthal, Tom, 186
Rotary International, 41
Rowntree, 93, 179
Royal Air Force (RAF), 12, 16, 125
Royal Artillery, 9
Royal Signals, 7, 35
Royal Society of Literature, 137
Rubenstein, Hilary, 155
Rubin, Neville, 64, 85, 138
rugby, 30, 36
Rupert, Prince, 31
Ruskin School of Art, 197
Russia, 92, 137, 200; Russian, 18, 44, 53, 101; Russians, 15, 85, 188

S

Sabata, Chief, 68–9, 83
Sachs, Albie, 64, 71–2
Sackett, A. B., 31, 33–4
Sainsbury's, 124
St Andrews, University, 210
St Anne's College, Oxford, 38, 210
St Antony's College, Oxford, 176
St Austell, xiii
St Christopher School, Letchworth, 126
St Cross College, Oxford, 212
St Giles, 38, 46
St Giles' Church, 208
St Joseph (Clare's boss), 93
St Martin's, Isles of Scilly, 129

St Mary's, Isles of Scilly, 131
St Pancras, 119
St Paul's, 46, 112, 115, 121
Salahi, Ibrahim, 162
Salih, Tayeb, 136, 149, 162–3
Salisbury, 47, 50, 58, 92, 106–7
Salisbury Plain, 207
Sambrook, Keith, 136–40, 148, 151, 158, 169, 174, 178–9
Samian ware, 21
Sands toy shop, 24
Sanlam building, 109
Scandinavian, 86
School Certificate, 21, 27, 33
School for Advanced Research Press, USA, 191
Scribners, 155
Scruton, Roger, 204
Sea Point, 67, 72, 78, 108
Secker & Warburg, 179
Second World War, 3–4, 31, 37, 167, 194
secondary modern schools, 26
Sedgeley, Mr, 30
Selassie, Emperor Haile, 144
Senegal, 92, 164, 193; Senegalese, 163
Senghor, Léopold Séder, 164
Serowe, 155–6
Sevenoaks, 7
Severalls, Colchester, 39
Shakespeare, William, 9, 42, 139, 151
Shandy (dog), 5, 7–8, 13
Sharpeville, 53, 62–3, 66, 93, 202
Sheffield, 8, 127, 172
Sheffield Smelting Company, 179
Shepherd Market, 177
Shepperson, Sam, 171
Shipanga, Andreas, 78
Shippeys, 24
Sicau, Chief Botha, 75
Sierra Leone, 25, 140; University of, 139
Silsby, Mr, policeman, 125
Sirte desert, Libya, 193, 212
Sisulu, Mrs, 103

INDEX

Skafell Pike, 129
Slade, Lucy (née Cacanas), ix
Slade School of Fine Art, 162
slave trade, 193
Smith, Wilbur, 165
Smithson, Alison and Peter, 37
Smithson, Simon, 37
Smuts, Jan, 75, 82
Sobell House Hospice, 190
Sobukwe, Robert, 53
Society of Friends, Quakers, 128
Soho, 126, 176
Somerset, 30, 194
Somerset County, 30
Somerville College, Oxford, 37
South Africa, 3, 7, 9, 46–7, 49–54, 56–7, 60–1, 63–4, 67, 70, 73–4, 76, 77, 80–1, 85, 89–90, 100, 106, 108, 110–13, 115, 117, 119, 135, 138, 146, 153, 157, 167–8, 199, 202, 204, 212; South African, 7, 14, 23, 27, 47–8, 54, 57, 61, 63, 66, 68, 70, 74, 76–7, 86–7, 105, 110, 112, 121, 146, 152–3, 155–6, 165, 175, 190, 204–5, 211
South Africa House, 57, 146
South African Broadcasting Corporation (SABC), 74, 76
South African Communist Party (SACP), 82
South African Defence Force, 82
South African Non-Racial Olympic Committee (SAN-ROC), 153
South African Railways, 89
South African United Front (SAUF), 70
South West Africa, 78
South West Africa People's Organisation (SWAPO), 76, 78
Southampton, 93
Southern Suburbs, Cape Town, 51
Soviet Empire, 44
Soweto, 89, 103
Soyinka, Wole, 116, 146
Spaak, Marielle, 41

Spaak family, 41
Special Branch, South Africa, 71, 77, 86–8, 90, 98, 100, 105, 110, 152
Spencer, Martin, 180, 187
Spencer, Stanley, 37
Spender, Stephen, 43, 205
Stallworthy, Jill, 118
Stallworthy, Jon, 114, 118
Stanyon, Miss, 18, 21, 26
Stationers' Hall, 46
Staverton, 11
Stellenbosch, 48
Stevenage, 115, 121, 124–5, 128, 172, 178
Stewart, Philip, 162
Stone, Lawrence, 39–40
Storrs, Sir Ronald, 24
Stott, Eulalie, 73
Stour, River, 48
Studleigh Priory, 38
Stutchbury, Hattie (granddaughter), ix, 1, 188, 210
Stutchbury, Martha (granddaughter), ix, 1, 188
Stuttafords, 9, 78
Styx, River, 3
Sudan, 125, 166, 191; Sudanese, 162
Suez, 43–4
Suffolk, 1
Sultan Nazrin Shah Centre, 211
Suppression of Communism Act, 52, 82–3
Swainswick, 195–6
Swainswick House, 197
Swanson, Douglas, 25
Swanson, Frances, 25
Swanzy, Henry, 34, 167, 208
Swaziland, 60, 68, 71, 73, 87, 90, 105, 152
Sweden, 101, 205; Swedish, 60, 199

T

Table Bay, 51, 96, 152
Table Mountain, 51, 64, 96

INDEX

Taiwan, 199
Taj Mahal, 19
Taj Mahal restaurant, 37
Tambo, Oliver, 82
Tanzania, 144
Tarr Steps, 20
Tate Gallery, 134
Taunton, 209
technical colleges, 26
Terbrugge, 104
Thackway, Melissa, 193
Thailand, 119
Thames & Hudson, 199
Thames Street, 116, 190, 197, 199, 210
Thames Valley, 199
Thames, River, 205
Theatre Royal, 155
Thomas Nelson, 8, 34, 73, 138, 181
Thomas, Akin, 142
Thomas, Dylan, xiv
Thomas, Joan, 43
Thomas, John, 10–11
Thompson, Pat, 34, 40–1
Thompson, Paul, 44
Thornhill Square, 133–4, 177, 179, 186
Thorstream, 103, 108, 110–11
Three Crowns, 73, 113, 116–17, 136
Tillings, 171
Timberscombe, 21, 209
Tinker, Mary, 195
Tito, Josip Broz, 194
Toronto, 108
Touws River, 84
Tower Bridge, 22
Toyne, Anthony, 135–6
Trafalgar Square, 57
Transcription Centre, 117
Transkei, 59, 64, 68, 70, 75, 83, 100, 101, 113
Transvaal, xiii, 54, 56, 66, 73
Tresco, 129–32, 195, 204
Trinity College, Oxford, 64
Tripoli, 50
Truro Hospital, 131
Turl, Oxford, 37
Tuscan, 43
typography, 49, 58, 60, 211

U

Uganda, 137, 188; Ugandan, 206
Umkonto we Sizwe, 53
Umtata, 64, 68, 83, 100–1
Umzimkulu, 69
Union-Castle Line, 25, 50, 93
United Nations (UN), 58, 90, 101, 200
United Nations Educational, Scientific and Cultural Organization (UNESCO), 76, 157, 191, 212
United Party, South Africa, 52, 73, 80
United States, xiv, 15, 18, 85, 179, 182, 185; *see also* America
University of California Press, 182, 191
University of Nigeria, 141
Unwin, Vicky, 137, 168, 209
Upstate New York, 184
Uys, Stanley, 61

V

van den Berghe, Major, 71
Van Gogh, Vincent, 7
van Rensburg, Patrick, 156
van Riebeeck, Jan, 51
van Zwannenburg, Roger, 187
Vancouver, 177
V-E Day, 18
Venda, 104
Venice, 173
Vermont, 114
Verwoerd, Hendrik, 57, 71, 81, 99
Victoria Falls, 105–6, 187
Victoria, Cameroun, 92
Vienna, 195

INDEX

Vigne, Gillian, 51, 59, 98, 103, 108
Vigne, Lucy, 59
Vigne, Randolph, 50–1, 53, 59, 63, 65, 68–71, 73, 80, 83, 85–6, 96, 98, 101, 103, 108–9, 111–12, 138, 212
V-J Day, 18
Voices from Ghana, 34
von Ribbentrop, Joachim, 20

W

Wadham College, Oxford, x, xiii, 34–7, 39–41, 43–4, 63–4, 68, 211
Walkern Mill, 4, 115, 122, 172, 179
Wallman, Sandra, 190
Walters, Tom, 71
Walton Street, 46
Ward Freeman comprehensive school, 127
Washington, 114
Waterford School, 73
Waterloo, 186
Watson, John, 182, 184
Weardale, xii
Welby, Justin, 202
Welwyn Garden City, 121, 128
Wesker, Arnold, 77
Wesley, John, xiii, 26, 28; Wesleyan, 36, 56
West Africa, 34, 151, 161, 193; West African, 139–40, 154, 191
West African Examination Council (WAEC), 139
West Bank, 182
West Country, 21
West End, 22, 50, 117, 177
Weston-Super-Mare, 14
Westwood, Kingswood, 29
White, Patrick, 57, 66
White family, 115
White City, 30
White Syke Close, 31
Whitehead, Gilia (née Slocock), 38, 210
Whitfield King & Co. of Ipswich, 23
Wilfrid, Miss, dame school, Daventry, 9
William Heinemann, 159
Williams, Shirley, MP, 125
Wilson, Anne, 106, 134
Wilson, Anthony, 106, 134
Wilson, Chris (Clare's brother), 30, 121, 123, 185, 207
Wilson, Eleanor, 129
Wilson, Geoffrey, 101
Wilson, Helen (Clare's niece), 123
Wilson, Henry (Clare's father), 39, 92–3, 117, 121, 128, 198
Wilson, Hugo (Lyn's son), 48
Wilson, Jeanetta, 129
Wilson, Lyn (Clare's brother), 48, 121, 129, 195
Wilson, Mr (Anglo-American mining company), 75
Wilson, Roger, 101
Wilson, Ruth (Clare's mother), 92–3, 117, 128–9, 198
Winchester, 35
Windsor Castle, 124
Winton, Nicholas, 14
Witwatersrand University Press, 185
Wolpe, Harold, 76
Wood, Freda, 1, 14
Wood, Graham, 14
Wood, Heather, 14
Wood, Lieutenant-Colonel Cecil, 14
Wood, Ralph, 14
Worcester College, Oxford, 38, 44, 197, 211
Worcester Reels Club, 38
Worcester, Cape, 84
Wordsworth, William, 151
Worku, Daniachew, 145
World Health Organization (WHO), 168, 200
World of Islam Festival, 166

Wren, Christopher, 39, 47
Wright, Edgar, 88
Wright, Frank, 23
Wright, Ian, 36, 133, 177
Wright, Lydia, 133, 177
Wuya, River, 140
Wynberg, 65

X

Xhosa, 56, 75, 113

Y

York, 93, 115, 172; University, 171

Yorkshire, 35
Young, George, 28
Yugoslavia, 194

Z

Zambezi River, 144
Zambia, 106, 144, 187
Zanzibar, 147
Zaria, 150
Zed Books, 187
Zewde, Bahru, 146
Zhukov, Marshall, 15
Zimbabwe, 107, 185; Zimbabwean, 176
Zulu, 76, 86, 157